Reflections on Spirituality in Pastoral Psychotherapy

Reflections on Spirituality in Pastoral Psychotherapy

CLARENCE LEON SIMS

RESOURCE *Publications* · Eugene, Oregon

REFLECTIONS ON SPIRITUALITY IN PASTORAL PSYCHOTHERAPY

Copyright © 2013 Clarence Leon Sims. All rights reserved. Except for brief quotations in critical publications or reviews, no part of this book may be reproduced in any manner without prior written permission from the publisher. Write: Permissions, Wipf and Stock Publishers, 199 W. 8th Ave., Suite 3, Eugene, OR 97401.

Resource Publications
An Imprint of Wipf and Stock Publishers
199 W. 8th Ave., Suite 3
Eugene, OR 97401

www.wipfandstock.com

ISBN 13: 978-1-62564-144-1

Manufactured in the U.S.A.

Unless otherwise indicated, Scriptures are taken from the Revised Standard Version of the Bible, copyright © 1946, 1952, and 1971 the Division of Christian Education of the National Council of the Churches of Christ in the United States of America. Used by permission. All rights reserved.

Contents

Preface vii

Introduction xi

1. Perspectives 1
2. Tools 13
3. Spirituality 17
4. Identity 27
5. Fragments 38
6. Awesome 48
7. Serving 58
8. Community 69
9. Growth 78
10. Longing 88
11. Hope 98
12. Postscript 108

Bibliography 113

Preface

In the poem "Lines Composed a Few Miles Above Tintern Abbey," Wordsworth gives voice, substance, and meaning to that most intangible of qualities: the *sublime*.

> "Of aspect more sublime, that blessed mood,
> in which the burden of the mystery
> in which the heavy and weary weight
> of all this unintelligible world,
> is lightened."

By this poetic measure, Wordsworth's lines not only reference that which is sublime, but address the very essence and mission of pastoral psychotherapy: the apprehension of spiritual mystery in our midst . . . the confronting of the unintelligible aspects of the world which surrounds and confounds us . . . the lifting of burdens worn too long like a yoke upon the souls and care-worn shoulders of those who appear at the counselor's door yearning for peace, grace and healing.

Just as the word *sublime* may describe the art and ministry of psychotherapy practiced at its finest level, it is also the most apt description of the profound spiritual reflections of C. Leon Sims. This treasured volume pairs the most grace-filled expressions of love for God and man with insights born of the author's incomparable clinical expertise. The result is a guide which nurtures, enlightens, companions and empowers both the novice and seasoned pastoral counselor alike, in a truly usable manner for which the profession has long yearned.

To God and grace was surely owed the gift of whatever inborn human potential I possess. But to Leon Sims' mentorship and

Preface

supervision is owed all that I am, and all that I offer to others, as a pastoral counselor and psychotherapist. Like a dedicated and compassionate gardener, he watched me grow and tended to my pastoral cultivation with the most subtle and nuanced skill. The result was an awakening to the realization that my professional maturation had at last been achieved, without my even being consciously aware of the mentoring methods through which it had been attained. Thanks to Leon Sims, I became, and remain, filled with the incomparable joy that comes from the practice of that unique compassionate care giving relationship that *is* pastoral counseling and psychotherapy.

As I continued the professional journey, I would sometimes experience surprise as I tackled complex and difficult therapeutic challenges with energy instead of fatigue, and with confidence instead of fear. On those occasions, I would often return to Leon and ask, "However did you manage to impart *that* to me?" Modest to a fault, Leon would disclaim any awareness that a particular lesson had been taught, or that an important theme had been explored under his tutelage. He would feign unawareness of how the particular, critical insight had been conveyed. But I knew differently. I knew the lessons came from him . . . from the core of who he was as a theologian, pastor, clinician and teacher. I knew that within the mind and soul of this beloved mentor were the "epistles" which would confer upon others the same lessons which he had offered up to me, if only they were reduced to writing. It became my fondest hope that this would occur, and that this volume would be penned. I believed it would create a priceless legacy—one which would give much needed voice and form to the discipline of pastoral counseling and psychotherapy as it continues in its contemporary struggle to define and maintain its identity in an increasingly secular world.

As Leon Sims and I entered upon our 14th year of mentorship and collaboration, I was privileged to witness the evolution of the book you now hold in your hand. Within every page—indeed, within every paragraph—the reader will encounter eloquent expressions of wisdom, inspiration and explanation, destined to be committed to memory and cherished for their timeless value. Within the unique pastoral counseling *matrix* which Leon Sims has created, the practitioner will find a truly usable system for approaching counseling challenges of every sort. And in each and every chapter, the reader will find something more valuable than ubiquitous, bland textual descriptions of clinical methodology. To be found, instead, is a complete and invaluable *thematic* anthology of pastoral and spiritual response to human suffering.

I congratulate all those who, because of their acquisition of this book, will learn from C. Leon Sims, as I did. All of his readers will find in the pages of this volume the highest expression of the counseling art. And, having done so, they are assured an encounter with the sublime.

The Rev. Dr. Chrysanthe L. Parker
October, 2013

Introduction

Mentors abound in a variety of "packages." W. B. J. Martin, of no impressive physique, overshadowed himself by the girth and depth of his care for people and insight into the Gospel. The stature of a person is not measured by feet and inches, but in the ability to influence other persons.

Dr. Martin came to Perkins School of Theology as visiting professor of homiletics sometime in the early 1960s. He didn't derive from academia, as one might expect. Rather, he was a working pastor in London until his writings caught the attention of leaders in centers of theological education. His little volume, *The Diary of Peter Parson*, is the compilation of his newspaper articles that caught the imagination of his countrymen long before he appeared on American shores. The articles, and thus the book, are his late-night reflections noted at the end of the day, personal and spiritual reflections on the events and experiences of his round of pastoral care. That volume, long out of print, to be sure, has accompanied me throughout my pastoral journeys and continues to claim a prized spot in my library. Martin's model has been chosen for the following pages.

The approach of this project has been to reflect theologically upon the occasion during and after an encounter with a person or group of folks who have attended and participated in some mental health setting. Some are counseling clients seen one to one; others represent groups within the clinical setting of a hospital system. Some of the clients appeared as outpatients, most of whom were counseled *pro bono* since the Center for Counseling and Wellness has been a ministry to the community. Others either were patients in the intensive outpatient services of mental health or were treated

Introduction

within the hospital. Names have long been lost to memory and time; thus, there is no issue with confidentiality. Nevertheless, fictitious names appear in this work.

These jottings might appear to be a hodgepodge of disconnected musings. And indeed they are, in many respects. They could be viewed as the pastoral theologian's homework, designed to prepare the seedbed for questions and opportunities to engage the client's latent spirituality. It should be noted that this work, based on personal experience, is couched in Christian concepts and language. However, as the paper progresses, representatives of all spiritual communities will find a sensitivity to spirituality in all corners of human experience. At no time have I set out to provide a theology in systematic fashion. The sections are only loosely connected. On the other hand, by arrangement and progression, the reader may find many of the essential elements of a thread or linkage throughout the work. Rather, I have attempted to reflect theologically on cases in ways that I haven't seen elsewhere. A large portion of this material was never presented, considered, discussed, or evaluated by clients in overt ways. However, this is a pastoral counselor who often referred back to various resources and consultations to think about a situation in a frame at variance to a psychotherapeutic one.

There are ample psychological materials available to diagnose and intervene in any of the conditions noted in this project. In practice, I often use brief counseling modalities. Cognitive-behavioral therapy (CBT) is a mainstay, and I resonate with Tan,[1] who has documented his spiritual adjuncts to CBT. I have been known to fall back into narrative modes, systems approaches, and deeper work with self-psychology precepts not far behind. In parallel as well, I routinely search for a spiritual frame or meaningful metaphor. I hesitate to extrapolate from them to make claims of grand therapeutic success with the clients noted here. These pages are illustrative of a process. This project might remind readers of Daniel Day Williams' "linkage" in the dialogue between psychology and theology in his *The Minister and the Care of Souls*.[2] In this instance,

1. Tan, "Use of Prayer and Scripture," 101.
2. Daniel Day Williams, *The Minister and the Care of Souls*.

Introduction

the counselor's theories and skills are assumed; they pale by design in the light of the theological exposition.

The reader will be introduced to a section titled "Perspectives," which sets in motion a review of the doctrines of revelation and epistemology necessary to assess an expectation of the sacred within the counseling context. The section on "Tools" describes the counselor's matrix of operation. The chapter on "Spirituality" is an exploration into definition and human connection. Thereafter, you will find a description of the process of human "Identity" formation. "Fragments" describes the spiritual and social conditions of human alienation. The "Awesome" chapter explores the options on which to base one's life, the one preferable being grounded in the Trinity. "Serving" develops a sense of call and vocation arising from Christology. "Community" speaks of a faith-filled people inspired by the prompting of the Holy Spirit. "Growth" describes how someone may turn from self-centeredness as an act of growth in kindness and care. Often love for relative or neighbor goes unfulfilled, adrift in pain in loss, yet the "Longing" for kinship remains. The section on Hope introduces thoughts on the in-breaking of God's Kingdom present and future. The Postscript attempts to pull together the major threads of the argument leading to a realization that sacredness is all around and all within.

Each case sets the stage and theme for the counselor's work. It stimulates a theological reflection that informs and energizes the counselor's ongoing engagement with the client. Each section thereafter follows the pattern of case presentation, theological research, distilled issues resulting from the client's progress, clinical verbatim, and case summary. This process has been chosen to address the central question for the pastor: Does the awareness and celebration of the sacred contribute to one's mental health and total well-being?

A note is appropriate about the use of gender references. The author is aware of the continuing dialogue and debate about stereotyping in contemporary discourse. As with other topics in this work, there are biblical roots. The mind turns quickly to Jesus's use of "Father" in the Lord's Prayer.[3] From this, and other precedents,

3. Matt 6:8.

Introduction

there has flowed a common use of the masculine reference to God, now in dispute. On the other hand, Isaiah's[4] "motherly" attributes of God have languished. I believe that the term "God" is somewhat impersonal in some contexts. I have chosen to use a first person pronoun followed by (sic) to signify unbounded holiness surpassing a human designation. On occasion, "God" is referred to as "he" or "she."

This work may be a resource for pastoral counselors, seminarians, and other professionals who have an interest in including spiritual resources for the healing of emotional and relational dysfunctions. Parish pastors may pick it up as a model for their own sensitivities to the life and gifts of the Holy Spirit as they provide succor and comfort to their parishioners. This project has been, in many ways, simply a means of clearing the mind, putting to rest some of the ideas about my work that cried out to be recorded somewhere in hard copy. Throughout the study, the following precepts have been at work at some level. These following professional "offices" are unique to the pastoral counselor:

1. The pastoral counselor will be a lover of humankind, whomever turns up at the door.

2. The pastoral counselor will be able to respond intelligently whenever a client introduces a topic in the realm of spirituality or religion, and will be able to avoid either undervaluing or dismissing the topic outright.

3. The pastoral counselor is prepared to perceive the unspoken issues or dilemmas, having the theoretical/theological structures "built in," and thus able to ask questions that move nearer the center of the presenting problem.

4. The pastoral counselor will be comfortable pursuing the client's questions that have spiritual overtones or components, expanding on them toward some definitive point of rest appropriate for the client.

5. The pastoral counselor will be able to synthesize conventional modalities of speech or thought with spiritual language,

---

4. Isa 66:13f.

producing a conjoining of meaning and power, thus leading toward inward healing and outward reconciliation.

I trust that these pastoral skills will be discernible as the reader moves through the following chapters.

My very special gratitude is extended to my wife, Mary Lou, whose dialogue and editorial skills have been invaluable throughout the many stages of the project. Additional thanks are extended to these colleagues who have provided encouragement, refinement, and readability of the contents. I include the Rev. Drs. James Pruitt and Ron McDonald, and the Rev. John Watson for their initial encouragement. Thereafter, Rev. Drs. Chrysanthe Parker and Hal Ritter have supported, critiqued, and counseled me toward a conclusion of the project.

These reflections are offered for the glory of God and the memory of W. B. J. Martin, with whom I was privileged to study for a season, and dedicated to my colleagues of the American Association of Pastoral Counselors.

1

Perspectives

Pastoral counseling has been practiced by parish pastors for centuries, since long before the psychological disciplines became prominent. Within the last several decades, however, the church has recognized a group of specialists who have specific training in both theology and the behavioral sciences. The field, previously dominated by clergy, is presently shifting to non-ordained practitioners who work in secular settings as well as church agencies.[1] And although there are practitioners who label themselves "Christian," there is a notable urgency to clarify requisite clinical skills within their ranks. The term "Christian" immediately connotes a viable theological perspective and, concurrently, does not assure clinical competence. Likewise, members of other helping professions are only recently incorporating spiritual disciplines. The very best presentation of this guild of specialists—pastoral psychotherapists—enriches and amplifies their clinical practice with spiritual sensitivity and theological articulation.

A review of various *perspectives* on natural and revealed theologies undergirds both of these practices.

What exactly is pastoral psychotherapy? I pose this question immediately in this project since several dimensions of experience are implied. Whereas "counseling" per se might refer to short-term

---

1. Townsend, *Introduction to Pastoral Counseling*.

Reflections on Spirituality in Pastoral Psychotherapy

behavioral change, "psychotherapy" implies alteration in personality reorganization. Pastoral psychotherapy may be viewed as a careful effort to attune the client's inclinations toward health and wholeness, utilizing contextually parallel modalities of story, myth, and metaphor drawn from faith traditions. Carroll Wise[2] has previously developed and refined this process. Ideally, pastoral psychotherapy integrates the best of sacred presence with counseling expertise. At the core of this project is the tandem of revelation (i.e., how God discloses) and epistemology (i.e., how God is appropriated and appreciated as a known reality). It honors two movements: recognition of the prevenient grace offered to all and facilitation of the latent health moving toward a horizon of renewal. Our common experience portends that tension exists—or, at best, a dialogue exists—between natural and revealed theologies. This essay develops these themes.

Although it is commonplace that the work of psychotherapy is done within a Christian context, it is apparent that counselors will interact with people of other religious orientations and, of course, many "nones" who claim no religious affiliation at all. It follows, then, that on the one hand, the counselor actively awaits some "aha" moment that signifies a sacred apprehension by the client. This event signifies the tenets of natural theology. On the other hand, a counselor may feel compelled to represent and speak for a belief system derived from revealed theology. That witness may be foreign to the client and may or may not enhance the healing process. I plan to explore alternatives with the prospect of developing a reliable theological posture that avoids the errors of either path solely taken.

Pastoral counseling and pastoral psychotherapy require a firm grounding that authenticates the term "pastoral." How these issues of revelation and epistemology are raised and settled impact directly therapy as an enterprise. The term "pastoral" immediately introduces the theological presuppositions a clinician may bring to the counseling process. How shall the sacred be identified, or discussed? A counselor may limit one's philosophical approaches to the communication of the Gospel story or scriptural passages.

---

2. Wise, *Pastoral Psychotherapy*.

Perspectives

Alternately, someone may lean toward a natural theology wherein God demonstrates activities generally as the world is and may be understood as such. The professional may adopt the concepts of Barr[3]:

> Traditionally, "natural theology" has commonly meant something like this: that "by nature," that is, just by being human beings, men and women have a certain degree of knowledge of God and awareness of him [sic], or at least a capacity for such awareness; and this knowledge or awareness exists anterior to the special revelation of God made through Jesus Christ, through the Church, through the Bible.

Barr, here, sets the stage for both revealed and natural theologies since they both emerge from the Bible. One may recall St. Paul's sermon in Acts 17. He must have sensed, as he was involved in life, that God has always provided a witness. In the Areopagus address, Paul supposes that people have a religious "instinct" and builds and proclaims on it. This assumption is echoed, of course, in his discussion of Romans 1:20f. Both of these references signal a dialogue—perhaps even a tension—between what is perceived to be God's general revelation in nature and the special revelation of God in the unique person of Jesus the Christ.

As Paul suggests, God has not left his creation without a witness. The vast range of human encounters with the *mysterium tremendum*[4] is chronicled broadly in the major religions of the world. Anthropological groundings suggest that human creatures have responded to divine revelation in a "piecemeal, discontinuous, and ambiguous" way since the dawn of consciousness.[5] Tillich[6] discusses the prophet's "ecstasy" as awareness of mystery, the ground of being and meaning. Sebastian Moore[7] proposes that human awareness of a relationship with the Divine, preceding the advent

3. Holder, *The Heavens Declare*, 147.
4. Otto, *The Idea of the Holy*.
5. Ward, *Religion and Revelation*, 83.
6. Tillich, *Systematic Theology*, 112.
7. Moore, *The Fire and the Rose*, 26.

of religion per se, is based on the deep consciousness of dependence on mystery as the very source or ground of being. More specifically, and coming to the fore, are these perspectives that strongly buttress a natural theology.

Stanley Hauerwas's[8] Gifford Lectures stimulate this lively debate. He takes on William James and Reinhold Niebuhr, and follows in the lineage of his hero, Karl Barth. Hauerwas's expositions helpfully mark out the divergent paths of revelation as perceived, discerned, and appreciated by students of theology. It is helpful at this point to identify how these paths diverge with the commentary representing each camp. Regarding *revealed theology*, Hauerwas introduces us to the position championed by Karl Barth. Other authors who echo Barth to some degree include George Lindbeck, John Milbank, Lesslie Newbigin, and Georg Reiger. Their comments follow.

Hauerwas[9] states that Barth regarded natural theology as "every formulation of a system which claims to be theological, i.e., to interpret divine revelation, whose subject differs fundamentally from the revelation in Jesus Christ and whose method therefore differs equally from the exposition of the Holy Scripture." The particular stance that Barth has taken in the *Dogmatics* is that theology cannot begin with human questions; rather, theology begins as an act of God in Christ and is, therefore, capable of giving faithful proof of our knowledge of God.[10] Barth contends that such "factual proof" is planted firmly in the Christ event. In Barth's[11] own words, we find:

> What the New Testament tells us of the reality of Jesus Christ is undoubtedly meant to be heard as the news of an accomplished fact, namely, that in the fullness of time it became true—and it was this that made this time fulfilled time—that once and for all God became Man and so His Word reached the ears of us men, and so we men

---

8. Hauerwas, *With the Grain of the Universe*.
9. Hauerwas, *With the Grain of the Universe*, 141.
10. See also Holder, who asserts and confirms this position, pp. 17–18.
11. Barth, *Church Dogmatics*, 165.

were reconciled to God. The reality of Jesus Christ is an objective fact.

Hauerwas, following Barth's lead, presumes that theology is not a business that begins with the multiform spaces in human experiences, but with the faith statement in Jesus Christ. Beyond him there is no empirical proof of God or his work. On the one hand, one believes that in Jesus God is completely and fully known; thereby Jesus is the Christ, seen functionally as Redeemer. If not, one is left to wander the philosophical field, searching for God in vain.

Voices of a more contemporary nature arise in support of revealed theology. The world, as is, may not be sufficient for a full understanding of what God is doing in the world. It is notable that George Lindbeck[12] claims that religious expressions are essentially culturally generated and conditioned, thus the experience of feeling, attitude, and doctrine. Further, Milbank[13] proclaims: ". . . the realm of feelings, affections, aspiration and experiences can no longer pose as a new site of universality, a firm 'base' in which to locate the religious, and on which to build theology." Lesslie Newbigin[14] would agree with the aforementioned perspective: "We do not argue from experience to the gospel. On the contrary, it is the Gospel accepted in faith which enables us to experience all reality. . . . What God has done for us in Christ gives us the eyes through which we can begin to truly understand our experience in the world." Georg Rieger[15] offers comments from a "liberation theology" perspective that spirituality is not so much a matter of our personal experience but a communal reverberation to what God is doing in the world through his [sic] son Jesus. These authors, quite impressive and erudite in their persuasions, post the critical issue of revelation squarely within the historical context of Jesus of Nazareth and the church's faith, and thus subsequent tradition, in him.

Theology begins and ends with the church's struggle to articulate her faith. However, the theological program is tested by

---

12. Lindbeck, *The Nature of Doctrine*, 39f.
13. Milbank, *Theology and Social Theory*, 382.
14. Newbigin, *Proper Confidence*, 96–97.
15. Rieger, *Theology from the Belly of the Whale*, 30, 114.

Reflections on Spirituality in Pastoral Psychotherapy

a pilgrimage through the valley of human experience; there is no way to avoid the thorny issues of anthropology and epistemology. Barth's position leaves one with a witness and also a feeling of disconnect with the common course of normal human concerns and a compartmentalized religion. Bonhoeffer cinches the matter when he charges Barth with "religious positivism."[16] This would be unfortunate, given that God has, as I know him, embraced every particle of reality, as entity, fullness of light, and invitation to dance.

In contrast, *natural theology* is introduced by Hauerwas by the works of William James.

Thereafter I cite some echo of the "experiential" side of the epistemology debate. Wildman and Brothers contribute from a scientific viewpoint. Matthew Fox seems to be fascinated with human sensitivities, and Daniel Day Williams, also, takes the conversation further. From these patriarchs, paths lead directly to contemporary frameworks for the professions of clinical chaplaincy and pastoral counseling.

Some say the work of William James set in motion two streams of dialogue: at once the discipline of American psychology, and the philosophy of religion. The latter is presented notably through the *Varieties of Religious Experience*. Bradford[17] references Smith (John E.), who calls attention to two factors that have contributed to the influence of the *Varieties*:

> At the turn of the century, the climate of opinion in both philosophy and religious thought was dominated by various traditions of philosophical idealism.... The emphasis was on religious ideas and doctrines and on the contention that religion could only be properly understood from within this perspective. Contrary to this reigning zeitgeist, James demonstrated that religion must first of all be understood in terms of the vivid experience of individuals who are struggling with personal concerns and crisis to which religious faith can and does provide an answer. James (1952) comments in the context of dialogue vis-a-vis Kant: The awareness that I think is therefore implied in all

16. Holder, *The Heavens Declare*, 88.
17. Bradford, *The Varieties*, 233.

experience. No connected consciousness of anything with that of Self and its presupposition and "transcendental" condition! All things, then, so far as they are intelligible at all, are so through combination with pure consciousness of Self, and apart from this, at least potential, combination nothing is knowable to us at all.

For James, the "self" is at the center of awareness and knowledge. With a stream of consciousness as his major premise, James would call it "over-belief," by which one seeks to hold life together and make some sense of it—to include some notion of God.[18] James's system implies that people must make an effort to deal with the "god-urge," and to move out from that in search of ideas, constructs, and strategies to talk about meaningful humanness. Making some sense of life and its mysteries one might call a metaphysic, as does Daniel Day Williams, in support of James's conviction.[19] In spite of all the postmodern verbiage about the end of all meta-narratives, every person must say something to him/herself about life, the source of knowledge, and its mysteries. He has a worldview no matter how mundane or inane, to which James makes a contribution.

Hauerwas[20] summarizes: James contends that there is a hard-wired urge in humankind to reach out, search out a god figure, searching for some sense of security and assurance. The result is a glorified form of humanism that neither supports orthodox Christianity nor affirms an honored place for the *humanum* in the context of creation. He does, however, identify the human urge to be connected to the Source of life, something that one might call the inner dynamic of spirituality. A man's religious faith, according to James, is "essentially his faith in the existence of an unseen order of some kind in which the riddles of the natural order may be found and explained."[21] Or again, faith amounts to the joyous conviction and assurance that all is well.[22] Hauerwas continues: "God is the natural

18. Hauerwas, *With the Grain of the Universe.*
19. Williams, *God's Grace and Man's Hope,* 10.
20. Hauerwas, *With the Grain of the Universe.*
21. Hauerwas, *With the Grain of the Universe,* 69.
22. Hauerwas, *With the Grain of the Universe,* 71.

appellation for the supreme reality, so I will call this high part of the universe by the name God. We and God have business with each other; and in opening ourselves to his influence our deepest destiny is fulfilled."[23]

In agreement with William James contemporary voices arise to herald the awareness of transcendence. From within the social sciences contributions are noted. Wildman and Brothers[24] have developed a procedure for dialogue between theology and science based on the principles and constructs of semiotics. They say "that Ultimacy is really showing up in ultimacy experiences. The manner of Ultimacy's showing up is a spectacularly rich and dense pattern of sign transformation that links enormous amounts of our experience together." In keeping, it seems, with the spirit of Wildman and Brothers, we have a range of words addressing the *numinous*, that part of humankind that bespeaks of a wonder and relationship set beyond our imaginations, often beyond our facility with words. Today both the harder and softer sciences are taking another look at mystery, wonder, and the sacred as dimensions of the totality of reality. The inquiry for our purposes, however, narrows down to the conversation between the social sciences and the major theologians of the twentieth century. Fox provides an illustration.

Matthew Fox's work *On Becoming a Musical Mystical Bear* brings a delight in imagination and wonder. He comments at one place: "The mysteries of life are by no means restricted to an esoteric sect, whether that caste defines itself by wealth, power, or religious affiliation. They are the lone bases for union among all men and women of diverse ideologies for they alone draw people out of their self-constructed universes. . . ."[25] I have chuckled to myself time and again about his quip that life is not a problem to be solved but a mystery to be enjoyed. That mystery of life is an idiom for the prompts from the depths of life toward spiritual awareness.

Is it possible that God has constantly and eternally provided a witness, given that he is God and none other, and also given that

---

23. Hauerwas, *With the Grain of the Universe*, 69.
24. Wildman and Brothers, "A Neurological-Semiotic Model," 412.
25. Fox, *On Becoming a Musical Mystical Bear*, 46.

Perspectives

the Old Testament is a continuous testimony of experiences of the Holy? On the other hand, Jesus is the definitive revelation of God, in concert with the revelatory work of the Holy Spirit who has tirelessly piqued the human awareness of his presence. We have come then to a definition of revelation. Initially I follow Ormerod and offer this quote: "Revelation is a hermeneutic process, i.e., a process for the uncovering and transmission of meanings and values which arise in relation to the life, death, and resurrection of Jesus of Nazareth.... The further process... is then carried on under the inspiration of the Holy Spirit. Thus revelation is God's self-communication in Word and Spirit."[26] The only addition one may make to Ormerod is the same "uncovering" process, under the guidance of the Spirit, that the clinician conducts when working with a client. The uncovering amounts to the discovery of God's loving work within human experience. Williams has developed a vision for the clinician that involves a revelation of the sacred through a provision of "sensitivity"[27]—perhaps not unlike prevenient grace—that must be appropriated through human intuition and critical reflection[28] This dynamic of sensitivity, conjoined between the human and divine, offers the surest promise for doing pastoral psychotherapy.

It is out of a Jamesian grounding, at least in part, that clinical pastoral education (CPE) and major schools of pastoral counseling have their foundation. These presuppositions are used whether attending an individual, a marital dyad, or facilitating groups. One's aim is to identify some resource for the mentally ill; to secure some tent-pole of strength that has been heretofore overshadowed by the depths of depression, etc. On occasion, this strength is identified as the spiritual component of human sensitivity to a sacred relationship or event. This presupposition, at once, identifies this writer as a child of the liberalism, to which James has contributed, that has been the intellectual environment of my time. There is a belief that God is at work throughout all corners of creation. It raises the questions whether there are other ways in which to address clients and

---

26. Ormerod, *Introducing Contemporary Theologies*, 49.
27. Williams, *God's Grace and Man's Hope*, 184.
28. Williams, *God's Grace and Man's Hope*, 46.

groups whereby they might reconnect with their Source of health. In fact, the argument here includes affinities in the "experiential-expressive" model of Bernard Lonergan,[29] which Lindbeck[30] disparages, as well as the philosophies of A. N. Whitehead and Charles Hartshorne's Process system.[31]

Kenneth Pargament comments in an opening page: "Spirituality . . . is interwoven into the fabric of the everyday. We can find the spiritual in a piece of music, the smile of a passing stranger, the color of the sky at dusk, or a daily prayer of gratitude upon awakening."[32] I am indebted to Pargament for leading the therapy profession so ably into a fresh purview of spirituality as a resource for healing and reconciliation. The first half of his book addresses the expanding body of research regarding the prominence of the sacred within the general population and that of the counseling clientele.

In a profound way, the pastoral counselor adopts Milbank's thesis that the church is the preeminent relationship builder[33] Each counseling client is not a prospect for a particular church, but each encounter in pastoral psychotherapy is a latent gathering of the *ecclecia* furthering the definition of persons. In my view, pastoral counseling epitomizes the "moral" and love-based atonement and is offered routinely as grace to persons in one's care. The work of

---

29. "Indeed the basic idea we are trying to develop takes its stand on discovering what human authenticity is and showing how to appeal to it. It is not an infallible method, for men easily are unauthentic, but it is a powerful method, for man's deepest need and most prized achievement is authenticity." Lonergan, *Method in Theology*, 109.

30. Lindbeck, *The Nature of Doctrine*, 31.

31. "Divine action makes our existence possible, with all its moments of joy and tolerable sorrow . . . and in addition gives us a rational aim and possibility of making wise, caring decisions in such fashion that, in the long run and on the whole, those we love, including ourselves and our human posterity, will probably . . . have better lives than if we decide carelessly or selfishly. Also, and in any case, whatever good qualities of experience we enjoy, or help others to enjoy, will be indestructible in the life, love for which is, so far as we understand ourselves, our inclusive concern. If there is any serious rival to this as an aim I do not know of it." Hartshorne, *Omnipotence and Other Theological Mistakes*, 122.

32. Pargament, *Spiritually Integrated Psychotherapy*, 3.

33. Milbank, *Theology and Social Theory*, 405.

the therapist and the sensitivity he or she offers is buttressed by the vocabulary of the church. From within the community of faith there has developed a vocabulary for speaking of God both near and far. The church has borne and carries forward the Gospel story of God's love for his creation and his creatures which focuses on the life, death, and living spirit of Jesus.

The Council of Nicea (325) began the processing of linking the action of Jesus with the action of God. Herein the doctrines regarding God were formally established. Trinitarian theology cannot omit the function of the Spirit in the word and work of Jesus within the original historical context—or the historical contexts thereafter. From this viewpoint the pastoral theologian adopts or adapts a theory of God present, or in conventional terms, the Holy Spirit. Although orthodox theists may criticize Whitehead's notions of God, his idea of a "consequent nature," ever creating and prompting each agent's growth, is congruent with this view of the Spirit.[34] I find the power of God not only in the grand, dramatic events of history, but also in the kenotic power of giving and sharing. God is dramatically giving throughout the history of the man Jesus, who appeared to the disciples and promised the return of a Comforter.

Disproportionate focus on the Jesus event as the central focal point, at the expense of the vigorous life and work of God the Spirit, is neither adequate theology nor effective therapy. Clearly, the notable works of the Spirit are what John Wesley called "prevenient grace," the unconditional love of God that preceded any person's awareness that he even needed it.[35] That grace, picks up the theme of Abelard's "moral" or love-based doctrine of atonement and prepares the ground for developing a sense of community. Grateful as we are, Milbank reminds us of St. Paul's notion that the church's business of mutual forgiveness and bearing one another's burdens continues the atoning work of Jesus.[36]

Being a child of the church, I have learned the nuances of the church's language. That language couches the basic experiences of

---

34. Cobb and Griffin, *Process Theology*, 48.
35. Outler, *John Wesley*, 33.
36. Milbank, *Theology and Social Theory*, 397.

Reflections on Spirituality in Pastoral Psychotherapy

the first priests, prophets, and disciples from the first days of the Christian faith. I also have learned that "church" words often point to and expose the deepest of human conditions and desires. The crucible for connecting the symbols of life are surely found in *clinical pastoral education* (CPE). CPE is the background for most clergy who venture from parish ministry into specialized forms of pastoral care, chaplaincy, or psychotherapy. That is certainly my history and my case. It taught me to become sensitive to the spirituality in the everyday human experience. Thereafter, I have set out to respond to the sacramental touchstones of the sacred in human experience alongside God's presence, most notably called the Holy Spirit. The following excerpt from Martin's *Diary* represents his viewpoint of spirituality, and the one that I champion.

> When I try to sum up in non-theological language what religion means to me, I find it inevitably shapes itself into two words—responsibility and belonging. I am never able to shake free of the knowledge that I belong to life, that I cannot contract out of it; and I am responsible, not merely to myself, to my neighbors and friends, but to God. And when I am true to these points, everything else in my life becomes significant and right. Nowadays I do not ask for emotional uplift; I find the more deeply involved I am in life, the more real God becomes to me.[37]

Both James and Barth could find a place for "responsibility and belonging" in the universe of their thought. Both responsibility and belonging are at the heart of one's daily life. My proposal is that the Gospel story, with its scriptural components, raises serious questions about and to the extent of human experience and the human condition. In tandem, and at counterpoint, the totality of human experience probes the biblical witness for truth, healing, and hope.

---

37. Martin, *Diary*, 42.

2

Tools

The conversation continues focusing on the professional abilities required for the performance of psychotherapy. The beginning place is an understanding of the client. There is within the client the inner impulse to become, to flower and flourish. The gardener, or, in this case, the therapist, probes the layers of soil to prepare, engender, and nourish the deeper thrust of becoming. A vehicle most apt and appropriate for evocation is the story, the client's story. Narrative therapy as a recognized technique adds significantly to the psychotherapeutic enterprise.[1] On occasion, other stories chosen from the Scripture record, parallel, prompt, or promote new insights. The language of the church, with its theological terminology, is enriching when carefully chosen. This connection between the client's awareness and the symbols of health and hope add powerfully to the curative prospects of pastoral care. Basically, the goal is to be as adept and articulate in spiritual and theological terms as one is at home in the counseling world.

Therefore, the counselor must come equipped with a certain set of *tools*.

I have contended that pastoral psychotherapy molds a narrative of revelation that God has interpenetrated all reality—existentially, continuously, and eschatologically—as a resource for client care. A dialogical tension must exist between two theories of revelation:

1. See Dinkins, Doehring, Goncalves, White, and Epston.

Reflections on Spirituality in Pastoral Psychotherapy

(1) an "immanentist" theory, which sees Godness universally available for human perception, and (2) a Christological theory, which ideologically and historically centered on the cross. The bridge between them is a robust notion of the work of the Holy Spirit. God is our contemporary, as he was also for Moses, Joseph, Peter, and Paul. And, if one comes from a Trinitarian position that the Holy Spirit is God's presence in us, then there must be revelation, as Martin says, for those of us involved in life. Norman Pittenger sums it up: "The Holy Spirit is working—he is taking whatever good has been seen and done, correcting subtly whatever error or evil has been present, and making everything serve in the long run toward the accomplishment of the divine purpose in the creative advance which we call the world."[2]

The discussion thus far has been theoretical and theological. Extending the notion that the pastoral counselor must trek through the harrowing events of human experience, I have included an illustration of pastoral sensitivity. Specifically, within conscious experience, bridged between memory of past events and the anticipation of future ones, four functions may be identified. These are described in the matrix below. From a neuropsychic grounding there are responses to both internal and external stimuli, as well as awareness of the energies of the Holy Spirit. These are the bases for developing a comprehensive approach to pastoral psychotherapy.

The goal in this section is to provide the reader with a descriptive matrix, useful for understanding and implementing a program of spiritually integrated psychotherapy. That is, there are various functions that invite theological language and discourse within the clinical setting. Gleaned from the ebb and flow of events with students and interns this matrix has emerged and proven helpful. These processes mirror the journey of Christian life from an awareness of discord or alienation; to an inner struggle; to a sense of being "right-wised"—made right in the eyes of one's self, others, and God; and then on to a sense of trust in life's ventures as being worthwhile and wholesome. In sum, these processes review a pastoral approach in detail moving jointly toward a spiritual and psychological reorganization.

2. Pittenger, *The Holy Spirit*, 107.

Tools

Although this model presents a fourfold intrapsychic dynamic and a fourfold dimensional process of role interaction, our focus is on the counselor/client interaction and change within the client. The "dynamics" noted are implicit and periodically nuanced or referenced in the casework that follows. The change model includes the following roles and relationships:

Dynamic	Client	Counselor	Supervisor
Anxiety	Unveiling	Holding	Assessing
Mobility	Exploring	"Midwifing"	Companioning
Integrity	Healing	Stabilizing	Contributing
Trust	Engaging	Encouraging	Evaluating

What makes these processes spiritual and psychological? We may see this dynamic through the lens of each participant's role in the therapeutic process. The *client* is moving through a series of psychic states leading to a re-engagement with life and, possibly a parallel religious journey to life. Within the setting of an adequate counseling environment, this journey leads the client through unveiling, exploring, healing, and engaging. The *counselor* plays a vital role in the relationship, providing the corresponding functions which are holding, "midwifing," stabilizing, and encouraging. Initially the client and counselor are engaged in/with the intrapsychic dynamics. On occasion a supervisor enters the arena, thus a tri-fold relationship appears around the client's prevailing dynamics.

I regard the beginning phase of all therapy to be at the point of *anxiety*. One might say that unveiling, as a function of anxiety, suggests the conditions of shame/guilt/alienation which may prompt a conviction and call for repentance. Conviction is a spiritual term indicating a heartfelt pain. The counselor's tasks are to accept and support during the first phase of the interaction.

Mobility connotes the processes of explorations into the range of ideas, feelings, and behaviors. Often, clients feel abandoned by God, alone and adrift in the sea of meaningless suffering. There can be an experience of existential drift. Mobility signifies the fullness of historical narrative along with emergent prospects for the future.

These are seed beds of new insight, awareness, struggle, and decision. The counselor's questions, comments, suggestions all assist the counselee to "give birth" to new options. Helping the client to become "unstuck," to move toward a new beginning, connotes the counselor's role of "midwife."

Integrity has to do with the reconstruction of self-fragments. In the healing and integrating process grace is received in the forms of value and worth as never before. The counselor, at this point, names, assures, and stabilizes emerging growth and health. Although the Holy Spirit is at work in convicting and prompting, so is the Holy Spirit the source and agent of reconstruction and sanctification.

Trust is a matter of risk. It prompts the client to re-engage with self, community, and life; only this time, he does so with the added resources which were not previously accessible. Faith being an active verb is a launching pad for life. The client has taken hold of forgiveness and or reconciliation to and for the former prevailing situation. The counselor's task is to personify the elements and extent of this quadrilateral through a holding, encouraging/validating, and confirming process. Now the counselor adds the quality of courage. He or she becomes a cheerleader for courage: "go ahead, take the step, make the change, live your life." Trust is a matter of risk, to re-engage with added resources.

At each step a supervisor, when occasion permits, has the opportunity to enrich the counselor/counselee interaction by being present, assessing the progress of the case, contributing ideas and options, and evaluating the change and growth program in motion.

The pastoral psychotherapist, utilizing these functions, will externalize and make visible to the client the previously tacit path of the Christian pilgrim. Something has gone amiss and "off the mark." There follows a yearning for quiet and reunion. Gradually counseling resources are at hand to make things right and new again. Finally, with great relief, all is well—really well. Hopefully this dynamic counseling matrix will assist the reader to ground the theological discussion to the specific events chronicled from the lives of flesh and blood folks who appear at the doorway of hope.

3

Spirituality

Bill Winfrey had called for an afternoon appointment, saying he would probably bring his parents along. The three showed with the elder gentleman in a wheelchair. By the end of the hour it had become clear that the elder gent, at seventy-nine, was senile but still trying to dictate the lives of his wife and son. Hard of hearing, irritable, and ill-tempered, he had sired a thirty-nine year old adolescent who hadn't been able to escape the gravitational pull of his parents. Every time he got a decent job and set out on his own life, he would "shoot himself in the foot," so to speak. He is now an expert at self-sabotage. Underneath one senses a seething rage—at his situation, his parents, himself? Is he replicating the anger of his mother, who can get away with it while he cannot?

Bill's experience assists us with the exploration of spiritually that is all about connection, with one's self, one's life, one's world.

This is a fractured family. At root, however, each person wants affirmation and connection. That is to say, they have "spiritual" promptings that their lives together could be much, much better. Spirituality is a core component of living in family groups. Any and all of our awareness of our complete human nature begins there. There, all the relationships, all of the subtle and overt powers, all of the yearnings to become, are born.

A similar case comes quickly to mind. Nikki is seventeen. She is *in* pain and *is* a pain. Her parents have dragged her into therapy for her acting out antisocially and sexually. The stepmom nags and berates. Dad, a military non-commissioned officer, suffers her rebellion against his expectations that she conform and aspire to being a "young lady." Nikki both loves her dad and hates him for leaving her mother and "shacking" up with this "woman." She finds all sorts of ways of making life miserable for herself and everyone around her.

The cases of Bill and Nikki bring home an introduction to the general topic of spirituality and the realization that counseling is largely concerned with it. What alienates us one from another? How does one belong? What are the conditions, requirements, and refinements required for membership in the human community? It is at the point of reaction and determination of one's true nature, in proper and meaningful relationships with others, and ultimately with God, that prods people into counseling. It is an awesome and wonder-filled event as a counselor honors and accompanies the search.

Although a dictionary definition of spirituality connotes whatever "attaches" to someone, Sorenson[1] suggests it is more like how one views life and/or is a way of life. My definition of spirituality is somewhat different. It is the *sensitivity* to, and *responsibility* for however the Spirit enlivens and energizes the person within one's life. Sensitivity is not a head trip; it is an intuitive awareness that life is beckoning in a way and calling one's name. Responsibility implies one's human capacity to make a response and the ability to guide the life forces in ways that are fruitful and productive. In some fashion it is a meaning, a holy one, that calls one forward. Cultivating those urges likely includes the rituals and habits of the heart that allow someone to stay in touch with the life forces within himself.

Bill and Nikki heard their names being called to something better than their experienced familial conditions, and something better within their own hearts. How does one become a free-standing, independent agent? There are always feelings of rage and acts of rebellion. Rebellion calls attention to the plight; it seldom solves the problem. Had Nikki or Bill been familiar with religious

---

1. Sorenson, *Minding Spirituality*, 24.

contexts, I might have shared with them the biblical story of Jacob. Recall, if you please, that he didn't enjoy his situation either. He heard God call his name in a different way, and he found a new person inside himself called Israel. Each of us yearns to be called by our right name which suggests that we are upstanding and autonomous agents before God and the world—so that we might come into communion with the world, through the vehicle of our highest and best self.

Usually all of this entails a "striving with God," a struggle which is often painful. Jacob[2] had his crisis at the River Jabbok, and Jonah[3] struggled with God to the bitter end. One man took a new turn and found God to be a trusted companion; the other, knowing the nature of God chose to avoid both command and fellowship. Many of us, even in the counseling chamber, have elected to run the "other way" from this struggle. Sooner or later life's sea monsters force us back into some program of doing what is appropriate for our time and our neighbors in Nineveh. This is not submission or coercion to be sure; rather it is recognizing the precise moment to choose cohesion—at the point of openness with one's true and actualized self.

It is not unusual for the counseling room to reflect and replicate the events of the Jabbok or a thrashing sea. I have witnessed the marvelous event of healing with "things coming together" for the client who has been battling her ghost, his demons, or their lost loves. Even patients with mental or emotional dysfunctions may look forward to an expansion of life and its goodness in spite of depression, panic, or other maladies that plague them. One says to them: "You are more than whatever diagnosis has been pinned on you." The mystery and wonder, even for them, is that health blooms along with whatever illness currently manifests and claims the center stage of attention. There is more to the person than the illness and its symptoms. Being sensitive to the life forces within, clients can expect to find the energy to continue becoming, move on, and

---

2. Gen 32:24: "And Jacob was left alone; and a man wrestled with him until the breaking of the day."
3. Jonah 4:2f: "for I knew that you are a gracious God."

developmentally confirm a unit of care for themselves and others. Williams comments at one place:

> Man, God's creature, is the being who finds every part of his experience linked with every other part. This point is sometimes made with the formula that man is a "whole." . . . What has to be recognized is the significance of the fact that every part of his being and his experience is linked actually or potentially with every other part. . . . A trivial incident may open the way for the first time to the discovery of oneself and of God.[4]

To be open to such discovery is a process that is neither disembodied, nor disengaged. The urge toward health is truly active even on those occasions when our grasp of life's issues are fuzzy and confused. It is a fact that wrongheadedness can endure even when the inner drive is toward wholeness and peace. For example, in a spirituality group once conducted by this author, one person proclaimed that she had embraced the Buddhist religion as a means of experiencing what she understood as the transcendent. Then the tenor of her comments suggested that she misunderstood transcendence, mistaking it for otherworldliness, which seemed quite odd and out of sync with her stated position. Had she mixed it up with platitudes more Platonic—that human beings are souls merely clothed in a material body which sheds off at death? Her comments and presuppositions did not satisfy the issue the patient had raised: she yearned for a way to be in touch with God, or to get in touch with herself to get in touch with God—or so it seemed. Human experience is necessary to teach growing souls the necessity and desirability of interdependence. One soul in one body relating vertically to the Almighty seems and feels cozy indeed. What if God doesn't think that to be sufficient for his relationship with us? In fact, the soul cannot develop into its robustness without engagement and interdependence on the relational, horizontal plane as well. What if that is a given among the postulates and axioms of the cosmos? As long as I attend to my self-centered and self-consumed affairs, all is "peachy." Enter another, such as a husband or a child,

---

4. Williams, *The Minister and the Care of Souls*, 27.

Spirituality

and life takes on a major challenge. So this life, on this planet, is an essential ground where self-centered infant souls get the opportunity to grow into Kingdom-sized souls by learning how to deal with the rest of the folks—washed or unwashed, as the case might be. It is not really a mean trick sponsored by a malevolent God. He [sic] wants his space populated by creatures who have this community challenge figured out. Maybe harmony in angelic choirs requires everyone hitting the right note, at the right time, doing it together. We have to learn how to do that!

One ponders what God is really up to, tossing us all into the emerging dynamic of human being, growing, suffering, loving. There is a devotional reading, I recall, chosen from Lamentations 3. It is a dialogue between what one suffers and what one hopes for. It is a beautiful passage depicting the difficult theological knot of how God brings his mercies fresh every morning, on the one hand, and how God alone is the source of suffering and hardship, on the other. This Gordian knot has never really ever gone away, nor has it been resolved. An attempt at this project is being projected by Keith Ward[5] and others around the old catechetical idea that the chief end of man is to glorify God and enjoy him [sic] forever. This concept, taken together with the idea of evolution, raises the possibility that God intends to develop a self-conscious human community. This opens opportunities through which God increasingly and existentially experiences the material world. To do that the human animal had to come up through the biological base, in union with the remainder of the created order, to be refined over the eons of emergence, and resulting ultimately into a creature that in *freedom* may choose to worship and love the Creator. In order to arrive at this amazing conclusion, the suffering of humankind is chalked off to the painful process of becoming. (I digress to insist that there could have been an alternate way!) At any rate, it is heartening to reflect on the quiet calm of the twenty-third Psalm—a good balance that suggests that God has shepherded us along the way into health and wholeness. He rises up to bless and ultimately perfect us. We merely have to do our part! How do we do our part? What are the

---

5. Ward, *God, Chance, and Necessity*, 175.

penultimate things we people can do to prepare for the precise at-oneness that defines our personhood, health, and happiness? Here is a list of a few exercises in spirituality which may help foster our preparedness.

One may begin the process by "brushing" up against the holy. A Wednesday night prayer meeting at the church might do it for some; a quiet moment alone suffices for another. For young people it often occurs in music, in physical movement, or a touch of acceptance. Any devotional (a moment where we devote the soul's attention to God's presence) usually happens in the rough and tumble of events, especially in relationships. The occurrence of such relational turbulence ought to be anticipated in the counseling room also, and these moments should be celebrated if they occur. Indeed, when Scriptural principles and actual experience come together, the pastoral counselor gives a name to event. Suddenly, a whole new step of spiritual growth has happened right before the client's eyes.

Matthew Fox contends that these rough and tumble events are precursors to prayer. He claims that praying is not speaking forth one's best ideas; rather, response to life's mysteries is the warp and woof of authentic prayer.[6] We discover, then, means for making each day a prayer day, a day in which prayer is seeking out with sensitivity the import of the events of our daily existence, however plain and commonplace. It would appear that a genuine spirituality begins with the heart of prayer born out of the struggle with interdependence in life. It takes flight and graceful form with the exercise, even the discipline, of looking closer at what we experience. Rather than retreat from the experiences life brings, Fox wants us to advance more confidently into them! We lift up prayers for those who will cross our paths today and pray that we may be sources of succor and mercy for a hurting and miserable lot. With the hurting and miserable we name the redeeming and healing urges in and around us.

Gregg Braden, at a hospital sponsored conference, proposed that the practice of prayer should be modeled after the Tibetan monks who pray their *feelings* rather than their *thoughts*. Examples

---

6. Fox, *On Becoming a Musical Mystical Bear*, 27f.

might be: "I delight in the sunset you have so bountifully provided," or, "I am fearful of what is about to happen now, O Lord." So should the whole world pray without ceasing, he says. Prayer should also, as shown by Native Americans in the New Mexico desert, draw on all of the senses to actualize a perfected, accomplished condition. Rather than praying for rain, the proper prayer procedure is to pray in thanksgiving for the rain event already completed. This modality in prayer delivers us from the indignity of begging God for "stuff" which neither dignifies either him [sic] or us. It also actualizes what we want to be, allowing people to contribute to something that seems so entirely beyond us and out of our hands—such as producing rain! Prayer is not merely a demand, but rather a praise for all things that life brings.

Since this is such a noisy, painful, and tragic world, one may always look within to find the infinite and a hope for internal rest. Calmness at the core is what provides the environment that one can extend, advance, and engage when folks sit with us in conference. Let us center and pray for inner peace, the shalom of wholeness and integrity in which all things hang together and with which no energies are lost or wasted. The writer[7] of the Hebrews knew something of a "Sabbath rest"—an inner peace and shalom. Jesus, the High Priest, after the order of Melchizedek, institutes the eternal rest beginning now in relation to the High God who presides over all space and time. There is a difference between being harried, rushed, and pressed—external stressors self-inflicted—and being calm at the core.

Let us never cease praying with gratitude. And when praying, never cease to remember the gatekeepers. These are the folks who opened the doors/gates for us along the journeys of life—parents, neighbors, teachers, and the like. It is likely that they made the difference in our personal relationships and critical life decisions. They enhanced opportunities for one's career. At issue is the fact that love was offered in this unique way: someone thought enough of us to provide a step up into another plateau of experience by simply saying in word or deed, "I believe in you." This might be called

7. Heb 4:9: "So then, there remains a Sabbath rest for the people of God; for whoever enters God's rest also ceases from his labors as God did from his."

true friendship. Prayer is a sure path to spirituality, so can *phileo* be far behind? All of us seek to be with others like us, so much in need. Over the phone, at lunch, and in laughter a lot of praying gets done. Friendships frequently open the gate to God.

Touchstones relating to the category of Integrity (see matrix, p. 15) involve healing on the part of the client and the encouraging contributions of the counselor. These processes are at work in the lives of Bill and Nikki. The counselor has the opportunity to "attach" to their yearning for wholeness and shalom. Their struggles provide the platform for the counselor to comment appropriately regarding the importance of being at peace in the core spot of one's being. He can affirm each person's feelings offered up in a spirit of approval and acceptance. Certainly he can affirm the client when he nudges close to recognizing the authentic person he or she chooses to be.

And finally, what can be said of Bill and Nikki? This excerpt summarizes the encounter regarding Bill's spirituality:

> Bill: I have obeyed them, doted on them, allowed my love to keep me bound to the folks way too long.
>
> Counselor: Has it been love?
>
> Bill: I thought so, but I'm not sure I have loved either them or me.
>
> Counselor: It has seemed something like "them or me?"
>
> Bill: And that is not right . . . not fair . . . doesn't even make sense, does it?
>
> Counselor: It is clearly a time to love yourself, so what does that feel like or look like?
>
> Bill: It feels good to have my own space, my own life. . . .
>
> Counselor: I believe that you are struggling right on the edge of seeing that fairness with your parents begin with your accepting and honoring some of your own needs.
>
> Bill: You mean the way I think and feel affects. . . . Whether I acknowledge and connect with me is necessary before I can connect and deal with them?
>
> Counselor: I believe you are on to something!

Bill: And yet these guys are my parents, even though they have dominated me. . . .

Counselor: And what would you like to do for them, or about them?

Bill: I want to . . . how can I say . . . I want to look after them, honor them.

Counselor: I believe I recall one of the Ten Commandments saying something like that. Honoring means that we don't give up on each other.

Bill: Believe me, lots of times I've wanted to scream, leave, hide. . . .

Counselor: How do you connect the dots . . . between honor and love at this point?

Bill: Well, there has to be room in all this for me to have my own space . . . my own life but still find ways to support them.

Counselor: You stay connected to them, but are not stuck to them either. You're saying, "Isn't that the best path to peace?"

Bill came to recognize his ability for self-affirmation. His self-negation hampered his growth and his family's health. He "stood up" to the "old man." He asserted that his father was no longer in a position to care for self and others. Bill was learning to own the power—and the corresponding privilege—of caring for both parents by differentiating from mom and sacrificing his dependent style of life. Bill moved out and last report is holding a job. He still keeps an eye on "the folks'" healthcare needs, arranges for transportation, and employs others for some of their daily "hands-on" care. He appears at peace with his authentic self and the role which it plays in relationship with significant others.

Nikki never made peace with the new "woman" who became her stepmother. She did, however, make peace with her dad, by understanding how partners' unhappiness can ruin a marriage—whatever their private details. Dad and daughter worked out an updated set of rules. Rules are freeing; they are spiritual because they set a pattern of expectations that make for peace. She had a hand in crafting them all. She calmed down somewhat and managed to finish high school. Nikki and her dad started a new life together based on renewed respect and accommodations. For her, rules are the rails toward interdependence.

Spirituality, in sum, might be reduced to owning one's selfhood while belonging responsibly to others. Connecting with one's oneness with self and his/her community, within a horizontal plane, includes the verticality of holy dynamics about us. This is the foundational stuff of spirituality. Pastoral counselors always make room for emerging and perplexing questions: What are the means by which the client hears his name called, responding to a desire to be renewed, while being sensitive to some of the wandering fragments of self lost in a world of relationships? Another way of saying this is: pastoral care supports the selfhood of an individual while supporting responsibility to the neighbor.

4

Identity

Patrick is coming in before I leave for vacation. He has a long history of being molested and abused; his ego structure is fragile; he is always fighting to keep it together. Patrick's emotional understructure is wobbly. It is scary. His penchant is overreaction. Whatever the issue, topic, or cause, he takes it to the extreme—and usually the worst. When feeling alone and dejected, he immediately thinks of killing himself—yet he is far from developing a plan. At a funeral he weeps hysterically for someone he barely knows. He connives to be liked, yearns "to make a good impression." The woman he married is astounded, confused, and emotionally distant from him. That is a challenge. Any time she diverts her attention away from him or their relationship he seems to panic. Any little rebuff from his spouse sends him into depression for hours, if not days. Who is Patrick? Will the real Patrick please stand up?

Patrick sets the stage for our inquiry into the formation of personal identity.

What is the etiology of this emotional dependency and threatened meltdown? Patrick's early history is marked by the lack of "narcissistic nurture" (i.e., a way of speaking of non-validation and marred by emotional abandonment). Further, he was physically and sexually abused by his older brothers and a neighbor. These life experiences left him emotionally adrift with few internal reference points or anchors to stabilize the inner life. He is now left in

Reflections on Spirituality in Pastoral Psychotherapy

the lifelong job of self-nurture, re-parenting himself as best he can with the support of professional help. Overreactions, inappropriate responses to stressors leave him mentally confused, emotionally in chaos, and everyone around him wondering who he really is. One might think of Edward in T. S. Eliot's[1] *The Cocktail Party*, struggling for significance. The search for significance and worth lie at the heart of Patrick's personal life.

In contrast to Patrick, Charlene came in last evening talking about Stephen Covey's seven steps for effective living, notably how everyone needed a mission statement to serve as the rudder of their lives. It is a happy stroke for her and others to heed what Covey has to say. A mission statement with goals avoids a lot of disjointed and disorganized activities that add up to little at the end of the day. Charlene, now fifty, has a real shot at focusing her effort and energies. She says, "I simply want to be honest and help people." Okay, in what way? With what or which goal? That mission statement, it would seem, is far too general. How about moving that down to something more specific, such as being the best employee, or friend, or parent that one knows how to be? Further, one might work productively and efficiently toward one's creative best. That might be more instructive about an identity.

Lots of folks never seem to be happy with who they are. Always being measured by someone else's yardstick was the focus on a two-year program of therapy for Trish. To feel that one has never measured up is a surefire route to depression and despair. Had she become whom she chose to be? That is a profound question for any of us. To be fulfilled is a human experience that is mysteriously but continually part of our indigenous spirituality. Has any one of us, whether Erikson, Fowler, Maslow, or whomever is addressing the issue, ever envisioned humankind to be as fulfilled as the Christian Gospel might lead us to believe possible? And so the quest goes on. By what standard or definition can we be measured to clear up the matter of personal identity? We'll quickly review salient psychological theory, turn to more philosophical themes, and return to theological constructs, each of which may illumine the identity formations of Patrick, Charlene, and Trish.

1. Eliot, *The Cocktail Party*.

Identity

From among the various psychological schools, I introduce this first section with thoughts on my own personality processing type, which is an INTJ. These familiar letters are at once associated with the Myers-Briggs Type Indicator, which is based on Jung's formative theory. The "types" are inclusive of the polarities of introversion/extroversion (I/E), factuality/intuition (S/N), thought/feeling (T/F), option/decision (P/J). Carl Jung, early in the twentieth century, departed from the identity theories and programs proposed by Freud and Adler to develop his own project based on "types."[2] This approach to identity assumes that one is considerably "cast," at conception, along the lines noted above with its various sixteen presentations. Jung's design, of course, does not preclude the possibility that one may grow and change, in order to promote the assets given at birth. These personality "molds" may provide hints for the basics in the ways that client present themselves.

Furthermore, development studies in young childhood include seminal works by Bowlby and Ainsworth on early childhood attachment. "Bowlby used the term 'attachment' to describe a relatively enduring bond that forms between two individuals over time in response to exposure, interaction, and familiarity."[3] They establish that an infant at first experiences the outside world as part of himself (self-object). Ideally, the persons who relate to him or her are nurturing, caring, attending—in a word, *empathic* to the child's needs. In the process of empathic interaction, a certain mirroring occurs—between infant and caring person, self-identification and self-esteem. The infant wants, then, to be with and be like the nurturing person, seeking to merge with him or her, or at least be like that one, idealizing the strength and power of the adult. The interaction affirms, validates, and lays the groundwork for the fledgling personal structure.

The development of the human infant is a fascinating story. Lee and Martin range over the work of Heinz Kohut and Daniel N. Stern. "These domains are the emergent self from birth to two months; the core self during the two-month to eight-month period;

---

2. Keirsey and Bates, *Please Understand Me*, 3–4.
3. Sable, *Attachment and Adult Psychotherapy*, 11.

the subjective self from the eight-month to fifteen-month period; the verbal self from fifteen months to about thirty-six months; and then the narrative self."[4] According to Stern, the differentiation of the infant from the mother occurs during the period between two and seven months.[5] Slightly in contrast, Kohut proposed that the self did not evolve as a coalescence of parts but was present from the beginning in a rudimentary form. The embryonic self is not a result of development; it is innate.[6] This stance allowed him to consider each self/person as an agent and thereafter could consider such issues as faith, freewill, and morality.[7]

Attention to Maria Rizzuto's work is appropriate for this setting. She disclaims writing about religion and recuses herself from judgments about the existence of God. Her concerns deal with the inner life of the developing child, in ways that prepare and set the stage for accepting ideas about the being and presence of God. When and how does the infant begin to "symbolize"—e.g., to embody something tangible that represents something so vast and mysterious? One answer might be found in Rizzuto's comment:

> The earliest manifestations are eye contact, smiling, and the child's fascination with the configuration of the human face. Eye contact in the context of feeding is the first indication of that exclusive human capacity to symbolize. The mysterious and indescribable experience of eye contact between two human beings respond to each other beyond the boundaries of need satisfaction. Through each other's eyes they enter the area of playing and transitional space.[8]

It is during this period of psychic development that experiences of basic trust develop.[9] With acceptance and relaxation (when object constancy exists), the child is free to fantasize. "They populate their transitional space generously with fascinating creatures—God

---

4. Lee and Martin, *Psychotherapy after Kohut*, 183.
5. Lee and Martin, *Psychotherapy after Kohut*, 183.
6. Lee and Martin, *Psychotherapy after Kohut*, 182.
7. Lee and Martin, *Psychotherapy after Kohut*, 181.
8. Rizzuto, *The Birth of the Living God*, 184.
9. Rizzuto, *The Birth of the Living God*, 184.

Identity

among others. The process encompasses the entire period that starts with object constancy and does not cease until adolescence."[10]

The sum of this discussion is that each child will grow and develop, having constructed a very unique sense of selfhood that is the product of the millions of miniature interactions with family, friends, and companions before the age of adolescence. At each moment and stage of development the individual may seek and search out those interactions that mimic early experiences, whether those experiences are validated, confused, or rejected. The individual gravitates to those objects, symbols, and relationships that mirror their early reality.

Moving from a psychological frame to a philosophical one, Hillman explores his notions of the *daimon*. Taking cues from Greek philosophy, Hillman proposes an individuality that springs from notions of a "preset" form or type:

> The acorn theory proposes, and I will bring evidence for the claim that you and I and every single person is born with a defining image . . . an angelic or daimonic intention, as if it were a spark of consciousness. . . . That the daimon has your interest at heart may be the part of the theory particularly hard to accept. . . . The entire image of a destiny is packed into a tiny acorn, the seed of a huge oak.[11]

Hillman's thesis holds that each individual has a "double," eternal and invariable, that hovers closer than our breath and heartbeat; one that knows our best interest, best calling, and pathway of life. The proposal is that the individual intuits this presence and responds positively to it. He disclaims genetics, parenting styles, or environment as the molders of one's experiences, development, and destiny. Rather, everything rides on the prior form, and thereafter the temporal formation that one may elect along life's pathway. Although seeing some affinity with Jung's work, clinicians may be unclear regarding how Hillman's concepts contribute to change in the client.

---

10. Rizzuto, *The Birth of the Living God*, 190.
11. Hillman, *The Soul's Code*, 11–13.

Reflections on Spirituality in Pastoral Psychotherapy

Let's turn now from philosophy to theological comment. Doud comments from the perspective of process theology:

> It means that a person is a history of microcosmic personal events. The direction of the route is not given once and for all in any one event, but each occasion contributes something to what is an accumulated directionality. Thus the making of the direction is itself historical. No event is completely bound by the direction of the past. Every occasion must contribute something to the direction-making process.[12] Our identity has to do with the series of events that makes us. . . . Identity presumes change, but it values continuity and stability.[13]

Process philosophers and theologians speak of microcosmic events. Based on preceding conditions, agents freely choose from the presented options, thus directing no predetermined future. The best choice lures the entity to maximize his/her trajectory toward fulfillment. Each entity/person may opt for the lesser choices, which, of course, affect the lifelong trajectory of the being, or in other words, a change of course in the biography. Daniel D. Williams, building on the work of Karen Horney, comments:

> . . . the real self is largely the potential of the personality. It is that which we truly can become if we are released from the distortion of our own false judgments, and from the blocking of our power to grow. The real self, therefore, is never identical with the actual self, for it is always more than we are at any moment in life. The real self is becoming.[14]

Williams has clearly laid the groundwork for much of the remaining development of the argument in this section.

While crediting William James and George H. Mead with opening the philosophical doors to a relational self, Stanley Grenz moves to connect the interior self with a sacred reality. He comments: "The corresponding linking of the insight of social psychology regarding the formation of the self to the human person

---

12. Doud, "Identity and Commitment," 392.
13. Doud, "Identity and Commitment," 388.
14. Williams, *The Minister and the Care of Souls*, 81.

Identity

emerges by means of the idea 'in Christ' that lies at the heart of the New Testament conception of spirituality. We are who we are by God's grace."[15] The psalmist,[16] Jeremiah,[17] and St. Paul[18] all profess the curious notion that God actually knew them each prior to their birth. Not only did God know them beforehand, he had a plan in mind, a predisposition for how this single life would be played out on the historical stage of his particular time. Actually process theology proposes the prospect of a "givenness" from the future that might be elected out of the freedom of each person. But God, in my view, could and does envision an option for us. A similar case could and should be made for the unique life of Jesus. As we will explore in a later passage, the Christ personage of the historical Jesus participated in the eternal plan of God's own sharing of himself with the world in the context of historical time. Each of these biblical characters believed that he had been uniquely set aside by God, ordained for a role, prior to birth. They believed that God truly preordained the possibility that each could play a unique, redemptive role in his historical context, giving credence to the freedom each enjoyed to choose another path. As a result of our understanding of the biblical genre, the Psalmist, Jeremiah, and Paul seemed to "fall into" a God given role. However, with Jesus, the choices were hard and painful, as the Gospel writers demonstrate. The Gospel writers certainly understood the prospects and the consequences of those terrible choices in the garden, leading to and through the cross to God's will.

On the one hand persons consider where and who they are in life and, on the other, they envision their future selfhood as a dynamic process. For Christians the whole idea of sanctification, leading from Gregory of Nyssa in the fourth century,[19] the Cappa-

15. Grenz, "The Social God," 90f.

16. Ps 139:14–15: "Thou knowest me right well; my frame was not hidden from thee, when I was being made in secret, intricately wrought in the depths of the earth."

17. Jer 1:5: "Before I formed you in the womb I knew you, and before you were born I consecrated you."

18. Gal 1:15–16: "But when he who had set me apart before I was born, and had called me through his grace, was pleased to reveal his Son to me. . . ."

19. Outler, *John Wesley.*

docian fathers, and thereon through John Wesley in the eighteenth, is *teleological*. It is pushing toward a fulfillment, intended at our conception and within the providential design, thus leading toward a "perfection in love" or a "Christ-form" within.[20] The point is, in sum, that some folks become more than they ever dreamed possible. Even with the heavy conscripting from one's family of origin, there is the pursuit and attainment of one's own bliss: the ability to love and be loved by God and one's neighbors—the ability to harbor the spirit of Christ within oneself.

What now can be said about the issues presented clinically by Patrick, Trish, and Charlene? For one thing, the clinician, by now, will have given up on the Newtonian world where determinative drives and forces collide with each other. A more viable psychotherapeutic approach would take its cues from Zohar, who suggests that human freedom is more like a leap of faith than a logical reason.[21] Or one could appeal to both Baron[22] and Cozolino,[23] who argue that psychotherapy is a gentle force for "rewiring the brain."[24]

We have argued that personhood is an interpersonal as well as a biological event. The person, therefore, as active agent may elect the succession of A, B, and C as momentary choices, thereby committing to a trajectory of life. That trajectory moves on course optimally, along with the choices that bode for the best outcomes for that individual. Patrick is seeking a center, Trish acceptance/fulfillment, Charlene direction. They remind one of the characters in *The Wizard of Oz*.

The matrix (p. 15) for pastoral care includes the dynamic roles labeled "mobility," where the counselor is working with the interrelationship of exploration, on the part of the client, and discovering mutual interpretations. Counseling supports the emerging being. Both counselor and client, hopefully, are open to emerging options, choices, and visions.

20. Outler, *John Wesley*, 119.
21. Zohar, *The Quantum Self*, 182.
22. Baron, *The Aging Escape Zone*.
23. Cozolino, *The Neuroscience of Psychotherapy*.
24. Cozolino, *The Neuroscience of Psychotherapy*, 307.

Identity

Let's listen in on the interchange between Patrick and the counselor:

> Patrick: I seem to be caught between a pit of quicksand or being shaken in an earthquake!
>
> Counselor: Nothing solid to stand on, huh?
>
> Patrick: Well, you know, I say things that I think people like, but then when it falls flat . . . .
>
> Counselor: There seems to be something missing in the way you project your ideas?
>
> Patrick: Right . . . and then I try to fix it by saying or doing something else just as stupid.
>
> Counselor: Let me try an image to see if it fits. You try to form your personhood to fit what you think the other person wants to hear or do? Is that close? (Implied and unspoken is Romans 12:1–2.)[25]
>
> Patrick: Yeah, I guess it is something like that. Like I want them to like me, include me.
>
> Counselor: How does that work out with your wife?
>
> Patrick: She says she has to guess a lot and respond to a lot of shifting moods, impulses, and weird activities. She stays frustrated and may be on the verge of leaving . . . like everybody does sooner or later . . . .
>
> Counselor: Can you recall a history of feeling left?
>
> Patrick: I have a lot of stuff we could talk about . . . like the time that I was left at school. I think I was in the second or third grade. Mother often picked me up or sometime I'd ride the bus. This time the bus left, and I waited, and waited, and waited. Everyone was leaving. Cars came and left, parents left, teachers left. Finally one of the principals called her to get me.
>
> Counselor: There's a lot of terror and panic in your voice as your recall this experience.

---

25. Rom 12:2: "Do not be conformed to this world but be transformed by the renewal of your mind, that you may prove what is the will of God, what is good and acceptable and perfect."

Reflections on Spirituality in Pastoral Psychotherapy

>Patrick: Somehow it just seemed like one more time that . . . one more time, I suppose, I get lost. I mean, what I think or want disappears.
>
>Counselor: Were you able to calm yourself when you were left at school?
>
>Patrick: Well, I was able to talk to the principal. I had presence of mind to ask for help.
>
>Counselor: That could be an important point for you. You see, you didn't just go to pieces.
>
>Patrick: I guess I hadn't given myself much credit for that.
>
>Counselor: So our project is to help you communicate yourself to yourself and to others more directly or appropriately.
>
>Patrick: Can you help me do that?
>
>Counselor: Seems like we just struck a deal around a goal for our next sessions. The Scripture speaks of being "conformed to the world." I'm wondering if that describes you and what other options are out there for you? Is that something you would be willing to discuss?
>
>Patrick: Lead on, I really need to find me.

Subsequently, in the therapeutic mix, my questions evoke recollections and memories around credibility, risk, and competence, since these denote one's ability to move from a center into the immediate environment. Power for counseling clients' renewal springs, as for people in all walks of life, from credibility. In other words, are you believable? Do people find you to be what you say or do? This issue is central to Patrick's search for identity. He had to acknowledge the gap between his overreactions and his intentions. Histrionics, not unknown among males, may be altered by viewing and accepting the behavioral dissonance and the underlying assumptions which underpin them. At the core of Patrick's person, however, is a cry for validation. From there on his journey to self-identity involves embracing the risk (insofar as his wife is concerned) of choosing congruent behaviors, and of facing the prospect of pain and loss, as well as validation and acceptance. After choosing one road, of

Identity

the two that divulged into "a yellow wood,"[26] there is grief over not having chosen the other. The great danger for counseling clients is failure to choose the greater good as the options come clear.

Trish is looking for a fulfillment, since she has a Christian background, and could hear Paul Tillich's[27] dictum that one needs merely to "accept acceptance" and move on. With God's grace and the gifting of formation in people, one may keep her anchor firm. That is to say, Christ's spirit is found "living in us." There is the key to all the self-worth one desires. It doesn't hurt, by the way, to continue to plumb the depths of one's inner experience seeking an identity with the Holy Spirit and marks of competence. Competence may take the form or pattern of Covey's steps or others more personally defined. Thereafter, identity involves applications of intention, energy, and commitment to one's better choices.

Counselors and supervisors should take to heart the central theme of Mitch Albom's *Tuesdays with Morrie*. Morrie, who is dying of ALS, says to Mitch: "Be present and really pay attention."[28] Being present and really listening is what counseling and psychotherapy entail. Surely, for the more seriously injured we provide emotional nutrients and validation. The attunement and empathy Kohut described seem to be the best medicines.[29] Thereafter, for the "walking wounded," it is a good plan to raise questions about their trajectory for life, and further, what empowers it.

---

26. Frost, *The Road Not Taken and Other Poems*.
27. Tillich, *A History of Christian Thought*, 162.
28. Albom, *Tuesdays with Morrie*, 137.
29. Rowe and Mac Isaac, *Empathic Attunement*, 72.

5

Fragments

Dr. Montalvo is a person who appears to be above suspicion. He is a father, grandfather, and respected member of the professional community. Yet, most of his days and nights are spent longing to satisfy the fires of sexual desire—with women other than his wife. He could write the book as the original womanizer, a "dead ringer" for the central character in the movie *Alfie*. He will plot, stalk, strategize, and seduce. Part of the excitement is in the conquest of women. At a young age he learned the art of wooing them and bedding them. He complains about his boring and sexless marriage. With the wife being out of town, he is drawn back to the strippers and the satisfaction of the lusts he feels. Dr. Montalvo, age fifty-two, is on a pathway over the cliff—into an abyss, into nothing. Most of us in the "helping business" would conclude that Dr. Montalvo is a chronic sex addict.

Dr. Montalvo introduces this section, and in many ways epitomizes the lifestyle of someone whose spiritual life is in "fragments" and whose social life is in shambles.

Recently, Dr. Montalvo has become aware that his lusts will destroy him, his marriage, his profession, and his future. He claims he wants to turn away now from the baggage of sexual adventures over a lifetime. Can he? Will he? Does Dr. Montalvo really want to tame the licentiousness that dwells within him? "Attached to the tent pole of myself," he commented, "is an intellectual streak, leading to serious, intense preoccupations with abstractions. This applies also to sex. The sexual drive, active and celebrated as it has been since puberty, still haunts me and prompts fantasizing about erotic conquests even now in my middle age. Then, I act on the urges and women respond." Over a period of several sessions, the counselor kept puzzling over his client's porous boundaries and the "dark energies" that wandered through them. How could this be contained, and what was it that he wished to restrain?

Another case is that of Bev. Bev was Thursday's challenge. A stripper and exotic dancer, now reformed into a PTA mom, she is looking for handles to deal with her father. She never resolved his absence and abandonment. She has admitted that she is scared of Lilly, the devil-may-care double that resides in her petite package. She now gardens and tends house, but there is that alcohol-slugging, pot-smoking, sexual adventurer in there. She has set out to blend two women into one healthy person; what a project. Healing, for Bev, began down a track of gratitude for the gifts Dad gave her, finding a family of origin that made her proud even in her longing for him—lost as he was in Vietnam. It could be that every sinful urge is a vitality crying out for conversion and transformation.

On another occasion, Tommy came in saying he felt mostly through with his therapy, with two things remaining: his relationships with his stepdaughters and his mother. His mother is now actually aging and ill, not someone who is going to enter into family therapy with him. It was suggested, instead, that he wrestle with the "mother" within himself to include that part that belittled and humiliated him, that part of her that he still emulates or contests with energy and anger. The intervention opened a whole new arena for exploration leading to ventilation of powerful, rageful affect. He was not as complete, or whole, as he had thought.

These three clients were acting out in particular ways against a boundary. Whether acting out sexually, dealing with loyalties to harmful parents, or addressing one's internal fragments, the safety and shelter of boundaries had been ignored. Figuratively, these have been called "friends at the boundary" (i.e., friends "so-called" at the boundary of responsibility).

Reflections on Spirituality in Pastoral Psychotherapy

We explore at some length the initial issue: Dr. Montalvo's game of love, lust, and boundary breaking. The mystery that lies at the bottom of this story is the age-old power of the *sarx*—the flesh. St. Paul has a good deal to say about *sarx*: that it leads to sin and death and how it ultimately must be tamed by the renewing power of Christ. Sexual sin is an easy mark for disclaimers. Self-righteousness and bigotry cannot begin to compete for dramatic flair. Paul and James extolled the "double-minded" condition of humankind. The Beatitude promising to "see God" requires a pure heart, one that does not have a gaze directed toward multiple centers. This theme is played out more fully in Reinhold Niebuhr's commentary in which sensuality becomes enmeshed in the core problem of human pride (*hubris*).[1]

Although self-sufficiency, intellectual and moral elitism, etc., all publish widely the human condition that we name "sin" (i.e., to miss the mark of being fully human), I prefer to think of it in terms of inauthenticity, which implies a fracture at the heart of the self. This approach can be more biblically grounded, and we also find mythic echoes of it as well, as we see in Kopp. Kopp, suggestive of Hillman noted above, tells this ancient story: "In her wisdom, Aruru creates a double for Gilgamesh who will serve as his other half, his animal nature, someone who will break his pride by showing him that he is only a man. Each of us has such a shadow from which he flees. Each man is haunted by that specter of a double who represents all that he would say "no" to in himself. To whatever extent I deny my hidden twin-self, you may expect to see my personality twisted into a grotesque mask of neurotic caricature."[2] And so the point is made: There is some part that at once bedevils us and yet serves, a part that requires recognition and often redemption. It is part of the nature of things, part of the creation which remains essentially good, like sex, which is intended to bless rather than curse, for joy instead of regret. This divided and estranged "part" seeks integration into the broad daylight of all of our upfront affairs. Without a healing touch and hope, there is the yawning chasm of sin, evil, and death.

---

1. Niebuhr, *Nature and Destiny of Man*, 228.
2. Kopp, *If You Meet the Buddha on the Road, Kill Him!*, 32.

Dr. Montalvo is only a late-date representative of an ongoing human struggle for integrity and accountability. This libido energy is, however, not simply lust run wild and amok. Involved, as well, is the engine of life and the source of vigor and creativity. Psychotherapy is challenging him to redefine his creative urges. Rather than using all this energy in seeking sexual conquests, he may re-channel the dynamic to redefine himself. Perhaps he could become a more impassioned artist, a more present and loving husband, and a more present and disciplined father.

The case of Dr. Montalvo is emblematic of the contemporary spiritual condition. The yawning chasm for Western culture, I fear, is the spiritual force of nihilism. During the latter half of my lifetime, it seems that neither the existentialists nor the postmodernists have much to add to the prospect of healing at the heart and soul. One would do well to learn (second only to the Scriptures, of course), to stay anchored at the heart of classic Christianity. One needs St. Augustine, on the one hand, and Nietzsche, on the other, to fully grasp the depth of the void that will lurk culturally in the foreseeable years.

Some might say that nihilism is merely another name for evil. Whereas nihilism suggests an absence of being, evil connotes a powerful force. Both, nonetheless, lead to destruction and non-being. One might ask, "Has evil existed as an entity predating the existence of humankind?" That is Job, for example, who experienced evil not from his own doing but from some terrible cosmic power quite outside himself. In the ancient narrative, Satan has access to and talks freely with God; between the two a terroristic plot is hatched against Job. Assent and complicity lie then within the Godhead? This is an unfortunate charge to bring to a loving God. A more reasonable charge is that God has chosen a creation with a double strain of freedom and lawfulness; an admixture of possibility, unpredictability, and chaos. It was that way from the beginning, as the opening verses of Genesis imply.

In the natural world of God's good creation everything, sooner or later, deteriorates and ceases to be. This introduces the second law of thermodynamics which proposes that all things in a closed system will eventually run down (or, in a word, *entropy*). In some fashion, entropy affects every human being some way every day. Evil turns up in the storm, wind, and fire, but most harmfully in the realm of human interaction. Peck concludes: "Evil is that force, residing either inside or outside of human beings, that seeks to kill life or liveliness."[3] Evil may be seen as a reaction formation—a perversion of the good as Williams[4] concludes, with hundreds of faces and presentations, that arises from the quest for existential security. This charade fails, of course, and vulnerability, overreaction, pain, and suffering result and persist.

Choosing to extend his own fellowship, God elected to enact a community with temporal existence as an extension of his own glory and overabundant Being. God placed a law in the universe that leads to entropy. He also created a measure of freedom. All sorts of things can happen when all of creation is allowed to think, choose, and act independently. Humankind, some will claim, developed evolutionarily through every painful step from animal to man. At some point a creature became self-reflective, capable of conscious life, and therefore owned the capacity to fellowship freely with the Creator. Thus the door is opened for evil, spawning an accumulation of mistakes, misdeeds, and misused freedom eventuating in something that takes on a life of its own. Evil, then, was not a reality situated within the matrix of creation from the outset; rather, it emerged as a secondary factor from the failure of humankind to face the vulnerabilities of life, cope with them in faith, and extend to each and every kind assurance of care and keeping. As St. Paul would exclaim, sin and death have been the lot of Adam.[5] Each choice to misuse one's freedom to avoid the haunting specter of non-being increases the store of evil even more. From his particular point of view, Griffin states:

> God is not totally responsible for the evils that do occur. Each situation contains seeds for good and evil. God . . .

---

3. Peck, *People of the Lie*, 43.
4. Williams, *The Demonic and the Divine*.
5. Rom 5:14: "Yet death reigned from Adam to Moses, even over those whose sinning was not like the transgression of Adam, who was a type of the one who was to come."

seeks to lure the creatures to realize the greatest good that is possible in that particular situation. When the creatures actualize a lesser possibility, this failure is due to their exercise of power, not God's.[6]

Each person is his own Adam, hiding from his best self and thus from God. The occasions of man's failure to address and own one's faults and foibles seem endless. They open the door to creeping nihilism, already documented in so many ways.

Other instances come to mind, each involving someone struggling with a boundary between the inner self and outer self expression. One prominent professional person bemoaned his self-sabotage in this fashion: "I am disappointed in myself in some of my most critical meetings. I find an edge coming out in my voice, bespeaking resentment, even anger at the status quo. When I am not up-front with it, it sneaks out. I have an elitism that often goes unacknowledged and confessed. I regret that it sometimes shows in public. All I know is that in some crazy way my self-promotion is connected to my drive for responsibility and achievement."

Clergy are not immune from the dissonance within and between. Very often the recognition that relationships require a lot of work comes very late in one's life and career, especially as it occurs in marriages, families, and friendships. One clergyman commented: "I realize now that I have not been overly successful in building a network of relationships. Within the clergy fraternity there exists a subtle undertow of jealousy, suspicion, or distrust. This is not the most conducive context for building support over the long haul. Even though no overt offense occurred, a snub or cold shoulder withers budding hopes of familial sharing. Some folks open doors, and after one has walked through, they never return to greet or show appreciation for the kindness. Colleagues drop off the radar screen, so to speak, after an event, a service, a committee. "Well, it was good to work with you," and the connection can be lost until the next year or so.

A pastor commented to a colleague: "Okay, so I am really angry that Lynn ignored me in her time of crisis. Even when she

6. Griffin, "Creation Out of Chaos," 110.

needed support the most, was ill, and the responsibilities piled up; even then she didn't call on me for assistance." It may often remain a mystery why someone is relegated to the periphery of one's awareness, given the history of common values, commitments, and communities. Again, this alienation sets the stage for confrontation. This individual went on to say: "Yesterday, the meeting with Lynn was full of surprises. I confronted her with the fact that after a year I had no idea, not a clue, about how to relate to her or the church under her care." After some fumbling, she confided that she had been consumed to the point of exhaustion, and then came surgery. She had overlooked or forgotten how to be collegial and an old friend. She had also operated on half truths regarding one's interest in her ministry, making assumptions that had not been checked out. The confrontation between the two resulted in a new covenant to meet monthly for lunch to catch up, hear each other out, and make new pledges to friendship.

The professional landscape is littered with the tinge of hubris. Egotism or extravagant thinking leads to overfunctioning, taking undue risks with others' well-being, even practicing beyond one's level of training and professional competence. Within professional ranks the most seductive are the brightest and most alluring of the bunch. Part of being a good pastoral administrator or supervisor is to manage the grandiosity within the staff. It always makes sense to take the initiative to remain one step ahead of disaster, when a subordinate becomes expansive too quickly or inappropriately. As a good parent would do, caution is advised. Savvy supervisors caution themselves against impulsive judgments. Massive damage to counselees or interns occurs by creating narcissistic injuries. These not only may occur, but are, perhaps, inevitable to a small degree. This is the grist for the transference mill, and thus may be potentially therapeutically helpful. One must take care to provide avenues of remediation for novices who look for guidance from the experienced hands.

The effect that someone has on others is often understated and stunning. It is also clear that a mark of Christian maturity—at the very core of spirituality—is to be aware of how one's own behavior affects those around us. This is a worthy goal to be sure, and one

Fragments

that may take a lifetime to master. One example is found in the simple matter of keeping commitments to self and others. There is the case of Frank and his spouse who came for marital therapy. He had a session mostly complaining about her. She came in alone, and the real issues of the marriage came tumbling out. Frank never could risk, given his self-image and self-importance, confessing the truth of their real issues. Other counselees dip their toes in the water for two or three sessions until the going gets rough, down to the painful parts, and they fly away. Some folks give up on either themselves or on the counselor, or both, if they are allowed to drift away untouched. A collusion (a tacit agreement) defends clients from future growth and the counselor from dealing with his contribution to the therapeutic interruption. The obvious resolution is to follow up on the failed therapy as an investment in reconciliation and continuity.

Someone was truly wise when they first observed that good fences make good neighbors.[7] Everyone requires limits. Boundaries are ignored, overlooked, or overstepped. From time to time I remember the chest that "lived" on the back porch at my grandparents' home on Lillian Street. It must have been filled with assorted stuff for housekeeping or gardening knick-knacks. As a small child I was fascinated by the "junk" that occupied the top drawer. I had strict orders to stay out! It was forbidden fruit. Alas, I—almost—never tasted that fruit, but I learned about boundaries.

We return to the case of Dr. Montalvo. He is working on both ends of the therapeutic process: the issues of anxiety and trust (p. 15). He is disclosing the depths of his pain and his problem while simultaneously becoming willing to engage those issues in the presence of the therapist. The counselor is providing a safe space, supporting the disclosures and confirming the person within the struggle. He is accepting and validating the conviction that until someone confronts his sin, there is no rebirth. Again, St. Paul[8] is the master therapist, who clearly defines and describes the heart and condition of humankind.

7. See Frost, "Mending Wall," *The Road Not Taken and Other Poems*.

8. Rom 7:15: "I do not understand my own actions. For I do not do what I want, but I do the very thing I hate."

Reflections on Spirituality in Pastoral Psychotherapy

Listening in on the case of Dr. Montalvo:

Dr. Montalvo: You know I have an office in the valley and am involved with a nurse there.

Counselor: There are opportunities for you everywhere, but then, some seem safer?

Dr. Montalvo: It seems that way when you are hundreds of miles away from home base.

Counselor: We could agree that deception is not a matter of geography, but of intent and integrity.

Dr. Montalvo: Oh, I agree. I am just describing the extent of my wandering—from family and, I suppose, myself.

Counselor: For a moment there I could see a parallel between your affairs at a distance and your internal self-distance—being afield from what and who you now want to be.

Dr. Montalvo: Guess you could say that. I do truly want to understand the gratification, the thrill, and then the remorse. What is that all about?

Counselor: I'd say that the remorse is a good thing! It suggests that you know deep down that something is not right. It is just that you are not using your power to change it. The excitement overrules the power. I'm convinced that an awesome power resides within you.

Dr. Montalvo: I have a lot of power, influence—and certainly ability to charm the ladies.

Counselor: That power, I suspect, is telling us mostly about a creative energy that neither of us really understand very well. Sexuality is creative energy. Right now it is unproductive in wasteful affairs. What else could it address, inform, produce?

Dr. Montalvo: I haven't thought about creative energy in a broader way. I mean applied to something else. Not sex. I am stumped!

Counselor: Your gratifications now lie outside the borders of your commitments. I wonder where else you could

Fragments

seize upon a sense of gratification—without the aftertaste of guilt?

Dr. Montalvo: I suppose that is my homework.

Our work, then, is to recognize, celebrate, and direct the inner life and power of Dr. Montalvo in some exciting new ways. Although absolutely refusing to align with a twelve-step group, he did make some gains across the extent of his counseling history. Insight and decision followed that made a difference, although a cure still remained on some future horizon. He came to see that his inner child, a forgotten, split off part of the self, yearned for attention and validation but was denied from nurturing figures. In the process of early growth his search for validation became sexualized, laying the groundwork for a later career in promiscuity. That structure in the personality thereafter both compensated and indulged his underdeveloped impulses to nurture the ones he loved. In a welcoming setting, the promiscuous entity did not need to be denied, but rather welcomed and truly accepted. He began to realize it dimly: eroticism is one's inner drive toward emotional connection and belonging. It was a fearsome thing, he admitted, considering the loss of stimulation and constant adulation from females, but it could be managed. Validation is at the heart of one's self-worth.

At least for one day at the time, Dr. Montalvo chose to eschew his former lovers, commit to his marriage, and hold his family intact. Sooner or later his affairs would have been discovered with the attending dark void of loss of self-respect, relationships, and finally his profession. In the course of things he learned to reflect on the gifts that mother and other females had showered upon him. With that came a deepening sense of gratitude. He says: "I should be grateful for everything I have. I could love my wife again, even though she is a bit plump." Much more could have been done, perhaps, to connect Dr. Montalvo's budding gratitude with a larger vision of spirituality. A goal, at least in the counselor's mind, was for him to value the sex event as the celebration and sacrament of the worth of the relationship he owned. It might not be the endorphin rush he yearned for, but rather an enduring and reframed event, and relief, confirmation, and covenant that Dr. Montalvo is on the brink of maturation, not far from the Kingdom of God.

6

Awesome

Morehouse is a twenty-year-old Satanist—or so he says. He believes in self-indulgence, as if that were a brand new idea. He turns up at my door, court ordered, at the end of a probated sentence for battering a female. He denies the battering. He is reminiscent of other teen cultists and so-called Satanists I have formerly encountered in long-term treatment centers. Having been traumatized, neglected, and likely abandoned, what do they do? They turn to cults for identity and community. So Morehouse says what he really wants to do is to live his life to the fullest, for life is short, he says, and who knows what then? He probably thinks that to eat, drink, and be merry is original with him. What, in fact, is really involved in "living one's life to the fullest?" For this young person the connection is made between the adoration and worship of all things "gothic," black, and sinister and a lifestyle of self-indulgence. The battering charge, the alleged act of violence, seemed to be the core metaphor for this young man's orientation to life. One acts as one pleases.

Morehouse—and Lester, soon to be introduced—present the awful choices someone might make on which to ground one's life, in contrast with the "awesome" interrelationship within the holy Trinity.

Lester's is a similar situation. My meeting with young Lester was the classic close of my work day yesterday. Lester is truly a sight. He is rebelling against his middle-aged, middle-class father by dressing "gothic": lips pierced, baggy black clothes. He is an intelligent kid, incognito with body piercing and weird dress. He is sabotaging his high school education simply because he treats it like a game. At the moment he rejects his father's intense pressure to make the most of his opportunities. Curiously, he enjoys learning (but only subjects he prefers), and he barely dabbles at science and math as play things. Acting is his thing and his passion. His other passion is helping out his friends. He spends blocks of time helping his friends succeed. Lester shares unconditional acceptance/ indulgence with others, in the manner of his fondest wish for himself at home. He is so into the moment, and yet whiles away the days and nights. One philosophizes about what life is all about at age seventeen. In that vein, it is easy to engage him intellectually even as he defends his behavior. Who knows? Perhaps this kid could be teased into reading Augustine! Could it be that he has to parade himself around as a disaster simply because his father nags at him and judges him? This father/son business is tricky indeed. Somewhere in every kid there is the burning need to be approved and applauded by his father.

At issue here, as one thinks theologically about these brash young men, is the center around which life is organized and intimate relationships are managed—some may call that "religion" while others label it "worship." These matters lie in the back of the mind and color how the pastoral counselor addresses the clients in the office. Tactfully and technically, cognitive behavioral therapy is the *modus operandi*, but the subtle thrust of the work is to confront the false allegiances—some have called them idols—and the self-destructive behavior that follows predictably in consequence. The entry point for successful work is to find the meaning of action. Action is not merely the behavioral pole of common counseling practice; it represents a central theological tenet due to its inner connection with thinking and feeling. Allegiance is a center of value. For the Christian counselor, that value is God. The problem in this case, simply stated, is false worship. It follows, therefore, that

Reflections on Spirituality in Pastoral Psychotherapy

some attention should be given to traditions, scriptures, or practices that suggest true worship of the one God and Lord of us all.

These clients set the stage for an inquiry into the nature of God and our responses to him. This piece appeared in a newsletter, and it was filed away for just this purpose. My colleague, a clinical pastoral education supervisor, commented along these lines, and it still holds true.

> When we begin to confine God specifically to a religious area of life, we are forced to turn away from the ordinary experiences of life in order to be touched by the gracious reality of God. Yet this is not the way for Jesus. The fundamental message of Jesus about God is that human life is the home of God . . . if it makes sense to speak of God at all, then we must be able to experience God in the center of our lives where we spend most of our time and expend most of our energy. To realize that God is there in the center of our lives at the deepest dimension of every human moment means that God is never far from us. To experience God in the depths is to be aware that we are related to a larger mystery within which we live . . . our relationship to God and response to God . . . cannot be relegated to special activities or special moments. Our relationship and response to God are going on all the time, whether we want them to or not.[1]

Neither of the young men mentioned in my caseload would recognize that there is a spirit or force that is worshipful in their lives. Their attention to the outer trappings of a culture (with its myths and rituals) speaks volumes, messages that they have yet to fully appreciate or articulate. The general message of the "goths" is that "I am centered on indulging my hurts and asserting my defiance against conventional society."

I persist in believing a wise old fellow who contends that we find God at the depths and the rigors of life. Persistently, God does not go away or leave us alone. Long ago Paul Scherer wrote in his little volume *Love Is a Spendthrift*, for the Wednesday following the second Sunday in Advent:

---

1. Gula, *To Walk Together Again*, 4.

The havoc that tears its way through human lives comes not of God's absence but rather of his persistent stepping out from behind every corner just at the moment when we undertake to sneak around it in our effort get to away. Never is it true that we cannot manage to find him. . . . I sometimes wish we would quit using that phrase. Always it is true that we cannot manage to lose him. That was Adam's problem, back there among the trees in the garden. It was Jacob's and David's problem. It was the problem the chief priests and the scribes had on Calvary: not how to find him, but how to lose him. It is our problem.[2]

But to speak simply of God may leave this topic inadequately explained. In what sense do we mean that God is with us, at the deepest dimensions? I record here touchstones for recall and confirmation. I credit one of my former pastors with reminders of Augustine's description of the Trinity of God as Lover, Christ as Beloved, and the Spirit as the communion between them. This reference lays the groundwork for a discussion of the one God who is a union and whom we experience as three presentations. Unfortunately folks tend to "balloon out" one or the other of the Persons. There is an undue focus on one to the diminution of the others. An example is found in another of this pastor's sermons where she addressed the baptism of Jesus and extolled the work of the Holy Spirit as the movement that carries us forth to do kind and loving things for God's world. Although she talked about the Holy Spirit as the dynamic of life and love, she could have helpfully connected the Holy Spirit with the enduring, creative power of God and as the constant eternal companion of Jesus. God, within the Godhead, cannot be viewed as constant or unchanging in an ubiquitous way. In spite of one's initial impressions in the letter of James[3] and some hymnody, God is in motion; God acts.

So what can be said further about God's stability and God's activity? Thus we are confronted fully with the Trinitarian formula,

---

2. Scherer, *Love Is a Spendthrift*, 7.

3. James 1:17: "Every good endowment and every perfect gift is from above, coming down from the Father of lights with whom there is no variation or shadow due to change."

Reflections on Spirituality in Pastoral Psychotherapy

alternative programs, and the subsequent debate. Most process theologians will not be startled with this action issue, since their whole system is predicated on the idea of process, change, and movement. Process philosophy, in my view, cuts a middle ground between fundamentalist doctrine (and/or dogma) and Enlightenment assumptions. Whitehead and his followers would posit some notions about God's transcendence and immanence, making room for God's intervention in physical and temporal affairs all the time, both big and small. They move away from the classic Trinity formulations seen in these comments. John Cobb says: "Process theism is sometimes called 'dipolar theism' in contrast to the traditional theism with its doctrine of divine simplicity. For Charles Hartshorne, the two 'poles' or aspects of God are the abstract essence of God, on the one hand, and God's concrete actuality on the other."[4] Hill and Mullen contribute: "In Whitehead's doctrine of God there are two characteristics of God's nature. One is called the primordial nature of God which does not change. God's consequent nature, on the other hand, involves God's sharing with the creatures of the universe the power of his being which allows them freedom and spontaneity."[5] Thus, in sum, God is constantly influencing human life wherever we are found.

Whitehead, Cobb, et al., suggest that God is creating each moment's opportunities (i.e., God "lures" human response into the actualization of what only lies on the edge of potentiality until chosen and lived out). This could be another set of terms for the ministries of the Holy Spirit. Humankind, as with the entire cosmos, is graced with mysterious gifts. The "prehensions"[6] of God's work are designed to lure the present condition into some new formulations. God—not limited by our concepts of past, present, and future—comes to us out of the future and beckons the present moment to engage by invitation. Those who respond do participate in the pregnant moment. This may not be far from "faithing" into the future (i.e., one risks the moment on the hope that something

---

4. Cobb and Griffin, *Process Theology*, 47.

5. Hill and Mullen, "Revisiting the Process Theology of Daniel Day Williams with Implications for Pastoral Care."

6. Schilpp, *The Philosophy of Alfred North Whitehead*, 42f.

new and wonderful could happen). That is to say, leaping into the future is a wager that a good God has something prepared, that is awaiting us and that will be delivered in good order.

Note that Placher contends: "Yet it is hard to image a 'binity' (i.e., a polarity instead of a trinity) sufficing for a Christian account of God. For one thing, the Spirit figures so prominently in the New Testament stories of Jesus that it is hard to set out Jesus's identity as God as being somehow apart from reference to the Spirit."[7] Placher writes, following the lead of Gregory of Nyssa (AD 330–394): "All three persons are engaged in all of God's acts; such a claim leads into the philosophical thicket of what counts as an 'act'? . . . One can define what counts as 'an act' for a particular purpose. . . . In the case at hand, 'becoming embodied in Jesus of Nazareth' is something the second person, but not the first or third person has done. It would not count as something all three persons of the Trinity do. But, if we think of the 'incarnation' as a divine act, then all three persons are involved."[8]

Other viewpoints are derived from the postmodern camp. Cunningham writes:

> . . . a relational perspective makes it much easier to make sense of certain elements of Trinitarian theology. It has occasioned a retrieval of the medieval insight that the three "persons" of the triune God are more fundamentally, relations . . . relations that depend absolutely on each for their meaning. There can be no child without a parent, but neither can there be a parent without a child: the two terms are tied together into a knot of mutual causation and interdependence.[9] Trinitarian theology (further) insists that a "person" is not an autonomous centre of consciousness, nor a radically private entity; rather, persons are necessarily woven into the lives of other persons. They participate in one another's lives, whether they realize it or not. In God, the Three are all bound up in one another to such

---

7. Placher, *The Triune God*, 137.
8. Placher, *The Triune God*, 148.
9. Cunningham, "The Trinity," 189.

a degree that we cannot really speak of any One of them without implying something about the other Two as well.[10]

Although I adhere to the Trinitarian formula when considering the Almighty, another conception of intrapersonal relationships could be as follows: The proposition is that Godness is actually a bipolarity with an intervening relationship, which is an entity of its own—the Holy Spirit. One might say that there is a deferment of one person to the other (Son to the Father/Logos to the Mind). And so, the parallelism ensues that, just as the Son is obedient or submissive to the Father in a sacrificial way, so the historical Jesus is sacrificially acting out the eternal relationship—i.e., the Spirit—between the Logos and gracious mindset of God for all things forever. Christologically speaking, therefore, humankind benefits from Jesus's "passion" out of obedience to God, and as the Christ, who is at once divine and human, reestablishes our relationship with the Father. The net result is that the life, death, and resurrection of Jesus epitomizes what has eternally gone on within the divine relationship, and coincidently, it is concretized once and for all in the historical Jesus, eventuating a singular event requiring no rehearsal or repetition.

The biblical (and thus faithful) historical view of God speaks of One who acts to create, redeem/liberate, and sustain. This "economic" view of God is taken as the basic interiority of God's own experience. Whereas God has been viewed as Trinity, I wish to affirm that witness in the following ways. The presumption here is that God is a relationship. An analogy might be: the human person is an independent self, who in specific ways and times chooses to act. The act is an objective fact yet connected to the actor, the person. The person views his act, owns it, revises it. Thusly, in the revision the creation returns to him as an integral part of his selfhood. Applied in such a fashion to the life of God, one might say that God is tri-polar. From the absolute Ground[11] of being, with the choice, will, and love to create, God acts in history. That objective action is seen most clearly in the life of Jesus of Nazareth. As the eternal Logos, the Scripture claims that all things "were created in

---

10. Cunningham, "The Trinity," 198.
11. See Tillich, *Systematic Theology 1*, 147.

Awesome

him."[12] In the Christ event, the resurrection signals the eternal state of God's relational reality. The creative work of God is not, contrary to the human example described above, to revise the work of Jesus, but to be present to the created order in every single occasion of Christ's earthly experience and existence. This work confirms the life and work of Jesus, moving on through the Spirit to persuade and lure human experience into the next best actualization of the occasion. This persuasion may be clearly identified as the Person and the work of the Holy Spirit. This Spirit functions doubly to lead us into life and to transport our actions and continuing reactions back into the very life of God. It can be claimed, therefore, that God too, is personal. He relates, creates, accepts and is affected by the choices, failures, suffering, and loves of humankind. In this manner God "suffers" when his allure is spurned by any of us—when the good, true, or beautiful is rejected by short-sighted self-interest. It is a rejection of God's love.

Alas, what can be said, then, for Morehouse and Lester? Clinical diagnosis notwithstanding, false allegiances or self-centered idolatries were identified previously as the prevailing conditions that we find in the presentations of Morehouse and Lester. If misdirected worship leads to life's dysfunctions, is there evidence of true worship that leads to life abundant? The review of the Godhead suggests that God creates and supports every moment and every being. He offers the actuality of the best from the myriad of potential choices available to everyone. The Spirit offers an alternate relationship pattern to each of these two men. In the dialogue below, the counselor is working in the patterns of anxiety and mobility (see matrix, p. 15) and attempts to support and confirm any client disclosures that might move out of self-preoccupation. What is "abundant" life for these clients? That is the issue before us.

We listen in on Morehouse.

Morehouse: So what exactly is this place?

Counselor: It is a center for counseling and therapy for folks who have issues, problems, various sorts of aches and pains.

---

12. John 1; Col 1:16–17.

Morehouse: Guess this is the right spot then since the court made me come, and it is a pain in the ass. That's for sure.

Counselor: So you are not comfortable being here and talking about yourself?

Morehouse: I'm doing what I have to do to stay out of the . . . jail!

Counselor: Well, since you're here, let's talk about things in general. Like, how's life going for you?

Morehouse: Sucks pretty bad since I got down on my woman.

Counselor: Help me out. Does that mean you are stressed out, pissed off, what?

Morehouse: Hey, wouldn't you be, catchin' her doing it with one of your bros?

Counselor: You're upset and angry 'cause she has been unfaithful?

Morehouse: Upset! I beat her little ass.

Counselor: Oh, you think there is a rule against screwing around when you are in a relationship.

Morehouse: I make the rules here. I call the shots about what goes down and don't.

Counselor: Seems like the court has got your attention. So, what all are you in charge of?

Morehouse: My life. I'm in charge. I decide and nobody else.

Counselor: You choose what is good, bad—kind of the center of the universe. You decide about your life and what else?

Morehouse: I am going to live, love, and have a good time any time and every time.

Counselor: I am thinking right now of what "abundant life"[13] might be for you? I'd like to picture what a more, complete, and pleasant life might be for you. Perhaps another community with different values, or maybe new rules—whole new orientation?

---

13. John 10:10.

Morehouse: Right now I just need to get out of this jam . . . .

Counselor: Did you think about what would happen if you whacked on your girl?

Morehouse: Didn't have to think . . . just did it.

Morehouse began evaluating the consequences of his choices, viz the court order had gotten his attention. He had *reacted* rather than intentionally *acting* in the event with his female companion. The goal of therapy thereafter centered on finding the inner drive of rage to retaliate against people and life itself. His inner core of hurt, shame, and helplessness continued as the triumvirate that ruled his being. His actions developed out of that trinity. He would be startled with presentations of the Christian doctrines of the Trinity; he was hardly prepared for that. He could hear that he was following the call and commandments of unruly, unholy ideas and commitments. Those principles weren't working. The counselor's role with this client was to bridge over, to mediate, between self-gratification and his infantile ability to consider the wants and needs of another. That alone was a big step. It opened the option that he could choose a civil management of anger and behavior.

Lester was a more hopeful case. He couldn't deny that he was his father's son and his father couldn't deny his offspring. The two together worked hard at communicating in language they both could understand: they belonged to each other. As Dad softened and talked about his own struggles to become a man, they found a vision: What would life be like in five years, or ten? What would they be about? How could they contribute to a long-term connection and make a down payment on that in the present? It all begins with a simple act . . . like perhaps getting up in the morning and going to school. Worship, one might conclude, begins with an awareness that oneself is not the center of the universe, and that others count. Thank God!

7

Serving

Larry usually comes in for routine outpatient visits addressing a pervasive depression. He, in fact, "came apart" in my office today, and I walked him over to the ER. He has just begun to face the awesome traumas experienced as a firefighter and emergency responder. He has witnessed the terrors that no human being ought to see, and now they are playing and replaying in his mind night and day.[1] The persistent gruesome scene is about a child caught in a house fire. His sense of helplessness and futility overcomes all the rational explanations. No human being could have done more than he, and his fellow firemen, did that night. In spite of all the medications and electroconvulsive therapy (ECT) over a three-year period, he is still in the throes of those horrors. His prior psychotherapy did little to alleviate the persistent night terrors and suicidal ideation. He will, however, never emerge into a measure of health without coming to grips with the ghosts of helplessness and inadequacy in the night. Yesterday, I believed that he might have killed himself.

Larry provokes us into asking, where does extraordinary "serving" come from? A serving vocation may derive from the model of Jesus who also served.

1. Clearly Larry is suffering from post-traumatic stress disorder (PTSD). A complete review of this condition lies outside the scope of this paper.

Serving

There are some folks who have an unusual, uncanny sense of responsibility and accountability for the well-being of others. The psychological construct that propels people into service is often internally dissonant; the sense of service may be self-serving, while simultaneously driving one to be a helper. How does one explain that? It could be generalized that help is not always helpful, as in certain dependencies. Helping, however, becomes institutionalized with policemen, firemen, soldiers, and of course social workers and clergy.

Larry's story rests back in his family of origin. As an older child, he was consistently conscripted to do a lot of tending and fetching for the younger siblings. This early training, conjoined with a certain temperament, conspired to lead him into adopting a service model. No one can definitively identify what prompts individuals to choose a certain occupation or profession. It is clear, however, that service prompted by early scripting varies dramatically from care and nurture offered freely. Perhaps a lot depends on the *vocare*, the inner call, to be, become, and follow not only certain patterns and lifestyle, but an inner reach for connection with others. Whatever the exact motivation was for Larry, he chose early in adulthood to be a firefighter and thereafter trained for the EMS. Prior to the horrid house fire, he had racked up attendance at an untold number of car wrecks, accidents, and other mayhem. Now, in his late thirties, the accumulation of stressors were boiling over, fomenting night sweats, flashbacks, dysphoria, and suicidal ideation. His wife was frightened beyond words and kept a keen eye on him. She would personally drive him into town for doctors' appointments and shopping trips. Even today, she paces the hallway outside the waiting room.

Larry's situation introduces very intense clinical challenges. For the pastoral theologian, it also raises profound queries into the doctrine of atonement, and its relationship to clients who see the counselor's help in dealing with inadequacy, and often unremitting guilt.

Of interest for the pastoral counselor is the underlying context of the client's personality, addressing his/her wounded drive to care for, to nurture, and in some cases to minister to those exposed to a violent world. That is a spiritual project as well as a psychological one. The ultimate model for those who serve is found in the life and death of Jesus of Nazareth. To his choice of service and his death we now turn.

Does care for others and love of service always require that one should come to die? In some measure, and we will explore this further, love always denotes a measure of inconvenience and occasional suffering. In Jesus's case the path of love led to death. Quite some time ago, C. H. Dodd said this of Jesus:

> He became obedient even unto death, the death of the cross. Obedience . . . the willingness to be commanded at every step by the will of God, without any reserve—that is what explains the strange double strain in the story: on the one hand, the inevitability of it all, like fate; on the other hand, the deliberation of it all. In death Jesus obeyed his Father's will, with an obedience which was a self-dedication, a sacrifice of self. That is, in fact, what is meant by Christ's sacrifice.[2]

This foregoing piece from Dodd prepares us for an extensive venture into Christology, and thereafter a doctrine of atonement.

A defenseless Jew was executed in cruel Roman fashion on an ignominious little knoll outside Jerusalem. It might be claimed that the crucifixion prestages and upstages the resurrection on the plane of existential consequence for humankind. The crucible of the shift in time, history, and eternity occurred in God's will even before the cross, given the doctrine of the *logos* according to the first chapter of St. John. Although St. Paul clearly states in Rom 10:9 that belief in the resurrection is essential, he also claims in 1 Corinthians 2:2 that he will know of nothing whatsoever than "Christ and him crucified." For me, the bottom line is found in the simplicity that real love (*agape*) often and inevitably requires one's sacrifice of convenience and control for the sake of caring for another. That existential fact is built into the warp and woof of reality based entirely on the forbearance of one Person to the Other within the Trinity.

---

2. Dodd, *Benefits of His Passion*, 12.

Serving

Let us review what others have said regarding the pivotal doctrine/experience of atonement. The September/October 2004 issue of *The Circuit Rider* is devoted entirely to the topic of atonement. Several commentators summarize prominent theories of this belief system. J. B. Green summarizes the traditional views: Christ the Conqueror—triumph over the cosmic evil (Irenaeus); Satisfaction—the cross as satisfying the debt owed to God by a sinful humanity (Anselm); and Moral Influence—God's love moving humanity to repentance and love for others (Abelard).[3] The Anselmian perspective (as noted above) is ingrained in American culture, and its hymnody and liturgy. Much of what we hear from radio, TV, or pulpit is still majoring in the substitutionary doctrine of atonement. The Old Testament culture spawned and justified the function of the scapegoat. The substitutionary approach made sense in that historical place in time, and that agrarian setting. It is still the major theme proposed by most fundamentalist factions in Christianity. But it hardly does justice to one's concept of a loving God. Abelard had the better view on life, love, and the involvement of God through the Christ to his community of children. Taking a step beyond Abelard, Williams contends that:

> Jesus's suffering has transformative power not merely as a demonstration of truth but as an action which creates a new field of force in which forgiven men can be changed. . . . Jesus' suffering becomes the very word and speech of love finding bodily, historical expression and creating a new possibility for communion. . . . We see in the suffering of Jesus a disclosure of the suffering of God. . . . God is involved in the history of his creatures because he loves the world.[4]

Suffering also has an active and a positive function in regard to the atonement. Suffering reveals a need, a difficulty, a longing, or a disruption. While all suffering may not be constructive, it may actually become sanctifying, when it exposes the truth about evil, sin, humankind, and the extent of divine love. In Jesus we see not

---

3. Green, *The Circuit Rider*, 4–6.
4. Williams, *God's Grace and Man's Hope*, 184–85.

the mere suffering of a person but the suffering of God for humankind. "What Jesus reveals on the cross surely is not that human love suffers while the divine love does not. What he reveals is the love which does not shirk suffering, and that love is God himself at work."[5]

Sebastian Moore's seminal work in Christology adds another dimension to the discussion. Beginning with the premise of each person's radical isolation, the existential withdrawal from the primitive connection with one's Origin, he tends to focus on the guilt that proceeds from this human condition. This leads his argument in the direction of guilt and its needs for expiation or satisfaction.[6] It is more helpful, attending to Moore's foundational position on human sin, to hold that Jesus's death—Jesus being the one entirely transparent to and obedient to, and at one with God—dramatizes God's love by participating in the most fearsome barrier between us and God, thus opening anew our communion with him [sic]. Moore's later work[7] simply explodes with soteriology centered on the cross. Giving credit to Rene Girard, Moore says that the "scapegoat" function, which Jesus voluntarily chose, reduces human fear that one will die at the hand of his peers. Fear is the pivotal term. Humankind harbors fear of a vengeful god, and being angry due to these existential conditions, rage and become angry at him [sic]. By contrast, Jesus, being transparent and intimate with God, chose to end all sacrifice in accordance with Hos 8:13. Jesus's death, then, became the pathway to the lively return (the resurrected one) to the disciple's midst, bringing forgiveness and communion when one might expect revenge and punishment from a vengeful god. Love, then, is the key to a relationship with God in this world and one that expects to be completed only in the mysteries of those realities that lie beyond the pale of our best imagination.

To sum up, one's Christology might run along these lines: God chose to involve himself in the human condition in the most extreme way. Through Jesus, God experienced death, as man, in one

5. Hill and Mullen, "Revisiting the Process Theology of Daniel Day Williams with Implications for Pastoral Care," 20.

6. Moore, *The Fire and the Rose Are One*, 123.

7. In McCarthy, *The Contagion of Jesus*, 27f.

of its most terrible forms. It may, thus, be said that Jesus, whom we claim to be God incarnate, has truly experienced humanness. On the other hand, God is immanently involved in all of human experiences, so why should the Jesus event be all that special or unique, since God's will and presence are uniquely involved in *every* occasion ("prehended," according to Whiteheadian thought). Jesus was indeed unique, because the occasion of the incarnation facilitated not just mankind's accessing information about God, but *God* acting toward and for mankind.[8] Prior to the incarnation someone might conclude that there needed to be one watershed event, one setting so graphic that all humankind could point to it and exclaim: "There it is!"

This is the overarching meaning of the incarnation. Although God is immanently at work through the Holy Spirit in all aspects of existence, he is preeminently disclosed in Jesus. The suffering of Jesus connotes profoundly the nature of God (i.e., the absorption of death, the confrontation with the fearful void—pure nothingness). God "inhales" that and takes it into himself. Almost as if God breathes—the *ruah*—he goes to this profound length plumbing, and exploring, for our benefit, the very depths of death and nothingness. As Stephen Travis comments: "Christ the Son, entered into and bore on our behalf the destructive consequences of sin. In him God took responsibility for the world's evil and absorbed the pain and destructiveness of it into himself."[9] Thereafter, the resurrection is the symbolic mode of speaking—if not the "exhaling" of the Almighty—about the eternal capacity of God to reconnect with all things, all matter, all being for all time and space to renew, refashion, and reframe the life and stuff of the universe. Within the complexities of human existence, God prompts and promotes the best in and for us. Therefore, is it surprising that persons are responsive to God's prompting for tending, serving, even suffering in behalf of others of our kind? We venture into dangerous gaps and depths for others' benefit and, in so doing, seek to be Christ to our fellows.

8. Cobb, *A Whiteheadian Christology*, 393.
9. Travis, *The Circuit Rider*, 9.

Reflections on Spirituality in Pastoral Psychotherapy

    H. H. Knight of St. Paul School of Theology reports that the Wesleyan perspective on atonement arises out of the doctrinal notions of the Church of England following Anselm.[10] However, Wesley added another dimension to Anselm's doctrine. The Wesleys, John and Charles, built on the sacrificial work of Jesus's regarding humankind's eternal destiny. The additional dimension establishes that salvation is a restoration not only to the favor of, but likewise to the image of, God; implying not merely deliverance from sin but being filled with the fullness of God—culminating in Christian perfection, love of God and neighbor. In other words, Jesus Christ is a story of justifying grace. Justification empowers, additionally, a life sanctified. Again, quoting Knight, "The goal of salvation is not merely to appear righteous through the imputation of Christ's righteousness, but actually to become righteous, to have the mind that was in Christ. We love God and others in response to God's love for us in Christ."[11] In these doctrines we find echoes of Abelard, Daniel Day Williams, and even Sebastian Moore.

    Having this mind in Christ bestirs our memories. The Eucharistic table celebrated "in remembrance of me" prompts a reexamination of the role of memory as one moves toward healing. Without memory there could be no celebration of the life and love of Jesus. The church holds that memory and carries it forward, generation after generation. The core of the memory is the act of suffering love, although the history around it might shift across the years. The text in John 6 expressly speaks of eating the body and drinking the blood, things we are so accustomed to thinking and saying. We also miss the scandal. What absurdity that postmodern people regularly indulge in an ancient rite dealing with blood sacrifice.

    On the other hand, we live in a world where bodies are daily butchered and maligned, whether in the form of physical, emotional, or sexual abuse. Violence wreaks havoc on the world as we know it. We have grown to accept trauma as normal. Contrary to mankind's inhumanity to mankind God eyes our bodies as his creation and sacred entities. St. Paul said it so well: these bodies are the

---

10. Knight, *The Circuit Rider*, 7–8.
11. Knight, *The Circuit Rider*, 8.

temples that God erects for worship. So as God, in Christ, considers our bodies as sacred, we may absorb the body and blood of Jesus Christ, and thus absorb as well all his graceful gifts to us. In this ingesting process we awaken to find across the table our family of origin and our contemporary neighbor who desires our relationship. In their presence and words, and ours, we receive validation, support, and comfort. Eating at the communion table connects us with the worldwide span of humankind—most of whom have little food or have to settle for the crumbs from whatever existence affords them. The Eucharistic table is laden with meaning and opportunity. It impels us to strengthen the community around the table by taking the kinship with others more seriously and kindly. Each time we partake of the bread and the cup, there should be accompanying warm, family feelings, certainly gratitude for being included in this fellowship. Surprisingly, we are all invited to God's picnic.

There is a connection that runs from the Eucharist to the sanctity of the counseling office. We work and rework along the stream of memory. Sorenson reminds us that clients come into counseling hoping to drill down into the genuine past.[12] However, memory is a human narrative, usually created and recreated with some event at the core. Memory is malleable and thus open to reinterpretation, even to include being the actualized altruism, along with the suffering that was entailed.

As a firefighter, Larry's memory was in the process of being reconstituted around the night of heroism, caretaking with that of his colleagues in service. For Larry, the kaleidoscope of PTSD haunts him daily. Over the course of treatment Larry's experience ran the gamut of anxiety/unveiling, mobility/engaging, integrating/exploring, and trusting/healing. He and I have entered into the long journey of seeking healing through revisiting the horrors he endured in the process of being a caretaker of the lives and properties of his neighbors. The counselor has provided a holding context wherein Larry could remold memory in safety and revision himself in other patterns.

---

12. Sorenson, *Minding Spirituality,* p. 51.

Reflections on Spirituality in Pastoral Psychotherapy

A pastoral counselor is aware that persons may be motivated into service as a mark of sanctification in the sense that the Christian is always moving on toward "perfection" in love. Love, the *agape* described by William above, is at work for both the client and the counselor. That plateau of completeness lies on the far horizon; it can never achieve perfection in human beings. The client's role is to value and cherish himself and his deeds, enfolded in the loving arms of God. The counselor, in like fashion, will offer the *agape* of skill and insight, knowing that his/her efforts will be finished within the grace of God. Larry could well have embarked on a futile search for "perfection in love" through caregiving, which can never be adequate for the day, or the horrors of the night. One of our conversations is representative of the unresolved conflict between Larry's need to serve the cause of "perfection in love" (atonement) and his inability to achieve "perfection of result" in service to others, due to circumstances he cannot control.

> Larry: I had a really hard night.
>
> Counselor: You have shared with me that nights are bad. What was new?
>
> Larry: I moved around all night, got out of bed, and flopped on the couch for a while. Often I get up to check the doors and the windows in the kids' room.
>
> Counselor: You're restless, almost motor driven.
>
> Larry: It just doesn't stop. I think I move around so much to just distract myself from thinking . . . What about this? . . . How about that? . . . What could I do different?
>
> Counselor: Talk to me about the memories, Larry. Is there one you could pinpoint?
>
> Larry: Yeah, I'm holding this little burned girl.
>
> Counselor: The awfulness of that memory seems burned into your mind.
>
> Larry: I can't begin to tell you how awful.
>
> Counselor: Let's walk back through the scene . . . all the sensory input. What do you remember of the night, sights, smells, noises . . . ?

Larry: Of course, it was mayhem. I don't even want to remember the smell . . . the night was alight with the fire. There was shouting and crying. There were calm, clear directives from the leadership. Thank God for that. We had clear direction.

Counselor: Can you tell me about all the feelings around that night?

Larry: Feelings. I don't even know where to begin. Scared . . . just scared. Scared that we couldn't get them out . . . scared that the roof would fall in . . . God, scared to death!

Counselor: Memories of fright, fear, helpless . . . in helping.

Larry: Bad memories, doc.

Counselor: And you were there. You were essential and present. I'll share another point of view: Your work, your fear, your being there models how all of us could be with one another. It makes all the difference in this world.

Larry: Well, yeah, I guess we made a difference.

Counselor: In fact, you—Larry—made a difference. You gave yourself, gave your best.

Larry never discussed at what point he got into the EMS business, nor what prompted his choice of vocation, although his history said it all. Likewise, a pastoral counselor may not speak of the theological underpinnings of his work with someone like Larry. In one's own mind and counsel, however, respect for the choice and the function of caring persons, even at the client's own expense, permeates the counseling room. That sets the context for empathy and renewal. Ah, one might say, "Larry, you have all the marks and characteristics of a Christian who is working out his 'salvation in fear and trembling'" (Philippians 2:12). And he could respond: "Well, what does salvation look like for me? Will I ever have peace?" However he might have responded, the acts of love and service reinstitute human life as sacramental. For example, when someone stoops to care for a child or picks up a broken body, it is done in "remembrance of him," in memory of the broken body and the spilt blood of the

Reflections on Spirituality in Pastoral Psychotherapy

Lord Jesus. Reconstituting one's mind, memory, and body after the model of Jesus leads toward a fulfillment of the *imago dei*. Throughout this therapy, and the passage above, Larry is struggling to move through the dynamics of Integrity and Trust (see p. 15).

Larry appeared to be making progress in his therapy and healing when it was interrupted by a move. That, within itself, presented another potential trauma for someone about to gain a foothold on hope. Unfortunately there is no happy ending in many of the cases in the work and ministry of pastoral counseling. We are left with the impression that the counselor must be willing to enter the traumatic material, companioning the client as a first step of care. Thereafter, the pastoral counselor honors the sacrifices offered and anticipates the rebirth of vision for a new life. Despite the counselor's own search to embody "perfection in love," and to embrace atonement to God through perfection in service to others, he must in the end be satisfied with the knowledge that he has sought to make a difference—and to accept that this grace is sufficient.

8

Community

Most of the usual faces appear around the circle at the Monday spirituality group. Extremely painful material emerges from the group members, on occasion. Among them is Teri, a thirty-two-year-old blonde woman, attractive yet with a weathered look. She describes her depression that gets worse before her period. That is just the tip of the iceberg. In a third marriage to an underpaid workaholic, she is a "stay-at-home mom" to a blended set of kids, his and hers, while trying to cope daily with the strains of family life. Underneath are the presenting issues: tales of a terrible childhood, being moved from pillar to post in a family with seven kids, parented punitively by an unstable mother, and an abusive stepfather. She was sexually molested throughout childhood. She denies being raped, except once; she says it was sort of a "date rape." Nowadays, she feels guilty for not protecting her siblings from sexual exploitation; that hangs in her memory. She has had bouts of bulimia and alcoholism. For a period in her second marriage she was a topless dancer. Now, too early for a young woman, the bloom is off the rose. As she ages she is fearful.

Teri is just the first of those sharing life's experiences with one another. A real "community" is one where the Spirit allows us all to unveil and heal.

Reflections on Spirituality in Pastoral Psychotherapy

Patricia unloaded the twenty-five-year-old burden of her shame and guilt associated with the abortion to which she submitted without a protest or whimper. This thing has fueled her depression and dissociation for years. All the doctors, medications, and all the king's horses have not been able to put her back together again. For whatever reason, perhaps in response to the impulse of the Holy Spirit, she chose to unburden herself of the truth. Many of the women around the circle, of course, rushed in with assurance that it was in the past and ought to be let go. Others suggested a memorial service for a finalization and goodbye. These "quick fix" suggestions are well intended, but not helpful, of course. No one grasped the intensity of how she continued to victimize herself, thus providing continuing power to those who raped her and those who shamed her years ago. Only when she is ready to cease being a victim will she also cease berating herself for the loss of that unborn child so long ago.

Several women have elected to disclose their sexual assault experiences. One by one, around the room, woman after woman admitted to being either molested or raped during their lifetimes. Some were coming forth with the dark secrets for the first time, after struggling with it in solitude for a lifetime. And with all such cases, the antidote is to begin to relive the horror in small pieces, and slowly detach from the pain with a reconstitution of self-awareness and self-worth. These are just a few of their stories, deeply suppressed or tightly locked in Pandora's box for years. Is it because society has deemed them hardly fit for telling in church? As the stories of shame and pain tumbled out, I kept saying to myself, over and over, *This group is the church that Christ came for, intended to be: a place where wounded souls come for healing.* Jesus would be here in their midst, asking, "Who touched me?" He would in kindness respond by saying, "Arise and sin no more." From John Deschner's "Austin Sermons," we are reminded that:

> . . . a congregation needs to give thought to how rightly to manifest the unlimited witness of God's love and reconciliation among men. Actually, this is the question about the composition of the congregation, and about its openness to those who embody the chief divisions of our time. Do

you see the point? The church is not called to solve all our social and political problems. It is called to do something more difficult: to create centers of community in the face of those social and political problems. . . .[1]

The church as a "center of community" is the theme for this section. It is a feeling, compassionate center distinct from its multiple architectural centers for education and erudition. The church (*ecclesia*) is defined in John (3:16f.) as a center where people gather not merely for "eating and drinking"; they gather around a special table defined by the words, "Do this in remembrance of me." Although there are several centers for doing good deeds by social and political entities, the church is an embodied human center that visits, feeds, and clothes; for having done these things, they are done unto him (Matthew 25). The Spirit-filled church is a center around which Patricia and Teri would be welcome. The world has wounded them; the Spirit of the living Lord can heal them. But for these women, the church, as they experience it, might be a very confusing prospect. The pervasive question is, Why doesn't the church, as a local agency of healing, reach out, welcome, and assist in the healing of women (and men) with such wounds, whatever the sort? It has everything to do with the confusion of many minds about the nature of the church, its mission, and its role as a metaphor for the Kingdom of God.

Someone told this story on himself, and as it were, also as metaphor for the church:

> As a boy I enjoyed having this particular friend over to play. However, one experience almost killed a good thing. The two of us couldn't decide best how to utilize a beautiful huge cardboard carton. Then we thought we had struck a bargain. I began fiercely to fight off the attacking natives as we made our trek down the Amazon. Then, to my amazement, my friend started selling groceries out of the bow of the cardboard boat.

To our continuing amazement, our friends in the church, those folks we thought to be so much like us, take off on surprisingly

1. Deschner, "Austin Sermons."

different journeys. In the same boat we're each on a separate pilgrimage. Amazing! Some claim the church is about worship. Others major in evangelism. Oh, the church is an educational institution. Yes, the church is and should be about a variety of expressions. Redemption, although often missed, is at the heart of the body of believers. However, as the ritual insists, the church is of God and will endure until the end of the age. At its best it will be the "barque of faith," the boat wherein disciples, all quite different to be sure, will yet respond to the call and wonder working of the Spirit. As disciples we indeed work out our salvation in fear and trembling—with no few surprises.

Even before social issues and political problems emerge, community building is no simple matter, always a gift of the Spirit. The Spirit struggles with us to bind us, heal us, for ministry in his Kingdom. At first discipleship means moving beyond warming the pew and dropping a few bucks in the offering plate. Basic discipleship is connecting with these fellow worshippers one meets on Sunday mornings; some will be fighting native attackers, and others will be selling groceries. Some feel closer to their quilting partners than their church members; some are more attached to their twelve-step community than the organized church. A key for attachment in both groups is a sense of openness, acceptance, and honesty. We need each other. St. Paul (Romans 12:4; 1 Corinthians 12:27) said it best: We are members one of another. The head doesn't say to the foot, I have no need of you. Like the physical body we are always working at being knit together for being an effective body working in God's world.

The church on the corner cannot and should not delve into the ministry of addressing the pain and problems of Teri or Patricia—at least not without the presence of clinically skilled caregivers able to create the proper context of confidence, security, and confidentiality. Local churches are ill prepared to provide skilled facilitation for people with extreme issues. But at its core, this redemptive work truly defines the essence of the church. The Gospel of Mark (chapters 2–5) launches the journey of Jesus with narrations of healing physical, emotional, and spiritual maladies. John Milbank makes this point clearly for our time:

Community

The logic of Christianity involves the claim that the "interruption" of history by Christ and his bride, the Church, is the most fundamental of events, interpreting all events. And it is most especially a social event, able to interpret other social formations, because it compares them with its own new social practice.[2]

This is the key to understanding redemptive groups in hospitals and homes where the healing work is carried on by doctors and nurses—and sometimes by counselors and chaplains!

Milbank also notes that the church has a "goal beyond the goal of generating new relationships, which themselves situate and define persons."[3] One might say in translation: The church of Jesus Christ provides a place to stand and a social context in which persons are able to risk and test their faith in love, thus given a standing or belonging. This in turn is the process in which personality is formed and individuals "become somebody." The conjoint mission then, of both family and church, is to provide a place to be, not merely to have biological subsistence, but a place to try one's wings, and under the influence of holy writ, respond to the work of the Holy Spirit in person formation, thus equipping the saints for ministry in the world.

Following Augustine, Milbank proposes that the church, within the wider context of the world's communities, is something of a colony in a foreign land. A parallel may be found in small and intimate units for the formation of personhood, viz the family, and the next step—the extended family, as per the *ecclesiola en ecclesia*, developed by Jacob Spener and the eighteenth-century Pietists, and the small group movement of John Wesley. The central mission of the church, then, is to allow, enable, and celebrate "church" as a community where the shamed and abused may indeed become "somebody" of worth and value. From this exploration into church doctrine, it is time to return to the clinical base.

Counselors routinely facilitate conversation around these groups and occasionally interject comment and supportive

2. Milbank, *Theology and Social Theory*, 388.
3. Milbank, *Theology and Social Theory*, 405.

suggestions. The pastoral intervention chosen that day with the several women drawn into a straggly circle was a simple drawing. It began with the drawing of a house-like structure on the white board. Participants began to guess: what it might be? It was, in this case, the barn and manger where Jesus was born. Conversation ensued around how it must have been a place of nurture even in that barren and rustic setting. That is, inside themselves, they could/should locate a spiritual home as a place of inner comfort and health. Where is one's spiritual home? It has to be at that place where once, at least, someone felt treasured, at peace, and connected to the universe of meaning. Hopefully, that is the legacy of every mother's child. But, alas, that is simply not the case. For the fortunate, somewhere along the developmental curve, every human being catches some glimpse of comfort and security. Without this base there can be no hearing of the Christmas story, no hope of accepting the Gospel of God's love; there is no Gospel and no God. It is easy, therefore, to allow all sorts of gods to rush into the holy place there to reign supreme—and evil takes over.

Sporadically, a few individuals voiced how they had been trapped in their own pasts, held in bondage to the abuse and terrors that underlie most of their present distress. Many, for the first time, realized that they have an inner core—a genuine true self—that has been hidden away within the shell of the persona. Now, that little person, child or adult, strives to emerge with a new being. Nicodemus, are you lurking around someplace? Could there be a conversion, a new vision of one's own self? Lee put it this way: "Psychologically we would easily recognize that it is expansive (as well as expensive) to love what is different, what is new, what is confrontational, what threatens our comfortableness with the familiar (in addition to loving what is easy to love)."[4] Some proponents would advise that to change, one must love oneself enough to risk.

How does the church of Jesus Christ deal with such painful problems as co-dependency, traumatic sexual abuse, and abortion? It could choose to revise its idea of mission—not as something far afield but as something in our midst, as near as the family down

---

4. Lee, *The Becoming of the Church*, 187.

Community

the block. It would truly be a new day if the church on Main Street could provide acceptance, space, and personnel to address needs around them. Worship of the real Lord moves out to love the neighbor. Ministry transcends chaplaincy to the "faithful" and extends to reclaiming the lost and wounded. For all those who clamor for a new day in evangelism, where the Gospel is proclaimed to the lost and spiritually dead, they are urged to recall that there was the Word—made flesh. And so the church's evangelism must be more than words only; it must be the Gospel incarnated in deeds for the lost.

But people will claim unwillingness to bare their souls. Or, they will wonder: what if we get in over our heads and do harm rather than good? The answer to these issues may be reduced, in a word, to *safety*. The church may and could prepare itself with persons trained to provide the structures, training, and insight to welcome the shamed, guilty, abused, and untrusting. The best example of this vision of the church is exemplified by the Celebrate Recovery program initiated by Saddleback Valley Community Church in California. Their purpose proclaims: "to fellowship and celebrate God's healing power in our lives through the 8 Recovery Principles. . . . We open the door by sharing our experiences, strengths, and hopes with one another. In addition, we become willing to accept God's grace in solving our lives' problems."[5] As Jesus so aptly demonstrated, the Kingdom of God is found as a gift between and within the communion of faith and love. It is possible, still, as Jesus promised not to leave us hopeless, that he has sent us a "Counselor"—yes, the power of God's own Spirit to encourage and console us.

Leading into the following verbatim, it is helpful to recall some particulars of the therapeutic intervention. Experientially, the pastoral counselor is building trust (see p. 15) by engaging with the clients and confirming their attempts to restructure their lives. He encourages each person's integrity by identifying an insight or affirming a new decision each might make. He is in the community building business, so to speak. As trust is developed within

---

5. From http://www.saddleback.com/lakeforest/carehelp/celebraterecovery/.

Reflections on Spirituality in Pastoral Psychotherapy

a group, it models and dramatizes the inner core of the redemptive community called "church." There is a latent *church* wherever there are people who believe, and therefore "faith," into life as being worthwhile.

One conversation is recorded here:

> Teri: I can't image what you are drawing on that board . . . lots of squiggly lines . . .
>
> Counselor: Sorry, I didn't go to art school. . . . You know I'm attempting to illustrate something you might recognize.
>
> Teri: Sides and a roof, maybe. Now a star shining. Don't tell me those sticks are, maybe, supposed to be animals. You've got to be kidding!
>
> Counselor: Sort of, I am kidding, but not really. Some of you will recognize a manger scene from Christmas books and stories, right?
>
> Teri: Actually I grew up with a manger scene. I had Mary and Joseph, wise men, angels . . . everybody was around the baby Jesus.
>
> Counselor: Can someone talk about what attitudes or feelings you might have when you think about the manger where Jesus was born?
>
> Susan: You mean other than it must have been a mess?
>
> Counselor: It probably was a mess and didn't smell very good. But it was inside from the weather, in some sense protected. It had a sense of peace.
>
> Meribel: I was once in a real barn with real cows. Smells of hay. Also sort of cozy.
>
> Counselor: What do you mean by cozy?
>
> Meribel: Cozy, you know, cozy is sort of being warm and comfortable.
>
> Counselor: Would you also add the word, safe?
>
> Meribel: I don't think of barns being safe, but I suppose it could be.

Community

Counselor: Where I'm going with this illustration is very simple. I think of the manger and the baby Jesus as a model of safety and peace . . . one that everybody needs on the outside in the world, but also inside one's own heart. Can you search around inside and find a place of cozy safety, where you are really okay?

Teri: You're saying that we need a manger inside our selves . . . in our thoughts and feelings?

Counselor: Perhaps you can find a little corner of your awareness, your own being where you feel secure. Begin by identifying some experience—perhaps long ago and far away—but now you carry it inside your being. Perhaps we can take up this topic again next week. For homework, think about what it takes to be safe in your life.

Teri and Patricia left the hospital setting that day still holding a past that demeaned and disabled. They cautiously verbalized the feelings about who they were and what they had endured. They were exposed, also, to a vision where they could risk relating to themselves in a healthy fashion and begin the trek toward relating to the community in a more productive manner. It was a mental health ward, the door was locked, no one intruded; there was no threat. It was an outpost of the Kingdom.

9

Growth

Barb came by to bid me adieu—so to speak. For weeks on end, it seemed, she fumed about her dissatisfaction with her life in SA. She felt isolated, disjointed, and lonely. The one thing that thrilled her was her weekly meeting with the Toastmasters group. She looked forward to the talks and really got excited with the thought of, and the preparation for, her turn at the lectern. Her checkered history was one of bouncing about from Texas to California and back again. At sixty, she still had the heart of a vagabond. I always suspected she was "on the run," hiding out from something or someone.

Is this really a holy one standing at the doorstep? Barb invokes a bit of introspection into the art of becoming better, growing in grace. Another word for it is "sanctification."

At the making of the appointment of this last visit she declared she was leaving—again. Having decided to make a major change, she felt the need to fill me in. Some word from somewhere either from the "toasters" or our conversations had triggered a dream, a memory. Now she had to go. At the heart of her decision was the need to care for somebody. She remembered a "little old lady" at the residential hotel where she lived for a while, whom Barb recalls with fondness. "This person was very kind to me," she says. "I'm not sure where she is now, or whether she is even still alive, but I need to go and find her." The driving force to leave is not only her love for Sacramento but her decision to spend her days seeking out and taking care of someone. The vagabond, "burned-out, sixties hippie" has finally chosen to plant roots—to quit running and hiding. Is this just another installment in her peripatetic habit, or for the first time, might this be a commitment to life?

What exactly set her in motion? I have come to speak of Barb as one of the Lord's "latent" disciples—although truly living out a program of service to others is quite distant from simply talking a good game. Barb was ostensibly moving in the direction of truly connecting with someone. Some mystery prompted her to care. This, in fact, is not so different from the conventional notions that Christian discipleship is hardly something that one intentionally, rationally, chooses. Generally, it is a response. Without a lot of fanfare it is useful here to claim a human capacity to respond to the movement of God's Spirit in our lives—even before one is convicted of the Gospel's truth. Spiritual descendants of Augustine, and curiously the children of the Enlightenment, will assert the facilities of reason to apprehend what God is doing the world. Pannenberg is one among us who claims (and contra the "religious positivism" of Barth) that "The reality of God has to be presented initially 'only as a human notion, word, or concept.'"[1] In fact, Thomas Torrence asserts that as human observers we approach sacred data with preconceptions.[2] Alister McGrath contends that all knowledge is influenced by how things are in themselves.[3] In sum, according to Holder's reading of Bonhoeffer, one's awareness of all sacred impulses are *praeparatio evangelica* (i.e., preparations for the Gospel).

It is somewhat unfortunate that the translation in Matthew chooses the terms "make disciples."[4] That has been the theme of untold annual conferences as long as memory holds and may imply, at least for some, a form of manipulation or divine "appointment" unaccessible to contemporary people. The Greek transitive verb *mutheteusate*, by contrast, suggests an *enabling* and implies becoming,

1. Holder, *The Heavens Declare*, 115.
2. Holder, *The Heavens Declare*, 142.
3. Holder, *The Heavens Declare*, 178.
4. Matt 28:19: "Go therefore and make disciples of all nations, baptizing them. . . ." (RSV). "Go out and train everybody you see . . ." (*The Message*).

Reflections on Spirituality in Pastoral Psychotherapy

which is to say, *GO*—assist or facilitate becoming! God speaks "GO" to each of us today, as he nudges and lures any of us into discipleship. As Bracken summarizes it, the divine persons of the Trinity

> [do] not order us to do what they want but instead seek to persuade us to do what is right through what Whitehead calls divine "initial aims." That is, they first communicate to us the power to make a decision here and now with respect to some future action, but they also offer us a lure toward what is better and away from what is harmful for ourselves or others.[5]

What may appear too hard and scary also could be the narrow path to a new being. It implies following, learning, loving, serving, dying—at least to one's self. Discipleship is a response to a call from the Holy Spirit who enlivens Christ within us. (I'll have more to say on this "call.")

There are lots of Barbs in the world focused on their own preoccupations—until something or someone redirects their attention. Whereas Barb claims some social graces and personal strengths, others have more obtruding issues. Meet Melissa, a heroin addict. She is an attractive person who also has a very bright and inquiring mind. "But for what?" she says, "do I have to rise each day—other than to seek out a fix? For Melissa and others of her "clan," life endures, even when living ceases. Is it only the spiritual giants of the world who are able to peer over the wall of their depression and despair, and garner enough faith and hope to inject a moment with meaning? How does anybody touch Melissa with a life-changing word? Is there a way to rewind the story of her life before she became a victim, filled with youth, vigor, and expectation? Twelve steppers say she will need to turn her life over, body and soul, to her "higher power." Narrative therapists encourage her to retell her story with a more positive ending. The Gospel story says that she is not alone in her struggles in life and what appears to be a dead end can, indeed, become a narrow way into the Kingdom of God. Melissa may choose to work the Gospel story into her story and

---

5. Bracken, *Christianity and Process Thought*, 21.

Growth

come alive, really alive. But, again, it will be a response to a call, a nudge, or a vision of hope.

For Barb and Melissa, and everybody else, salvation from a self-centered lifestyle or toxic drugs is every day's business. Growing in grace is a process. Beginning with God's work in Christ, we are invited to engraft Christ's spirit within us. In fact, God planted a stake in time, and from that event all history changed. Lives changed. If we accept Jesus's life and death as gifts for us, we too are changed. There is a curious dynamic flowing through the New Testament: it tells of turning and commitment—a crucial decisive act—followed by a developing love that flows forth into every quarter of personal act and deed.

I have claimed that this "making of disciples" is a Holy Ghost business, which is another way of saying that God is immanently engaged and involved in human life as well as the other corners of the universe. Process theology suggests that God opens every new instant with options and lures us to choose the maximum path for good and that of others. Moving even deeper into the human capacities from a neuroscience point of view, I turn to George Ellis. He speaks in terms of a "causal joint" that is hardwired into the human brain through which or by which spiritual contacts are made.

> This revelatory causal joint does not control what goes on in our brains in the sense of constraining our options, but rather offers us visions or intimations of how things are or could be, and how to act, experienced generally as preconceptual intimations or as an "inner light."[6]

I won't linger over the details of his argument, based on his background in mathematics and quantum physics. Suffice it to say that the theological presuppositions of how people alter life's course have biological as well as cultural and spiritual components. This writer proposes here that this spiritual option remains open and responsive, although dormant on occasion, regardless of the totality of a person's condition.

What has obstructed either Barb or Melissa from hearing the Gospel's call and responding with a life of commitment,

---

6. Ellis, "Intimations of Transcendence," 471.

responsibility, and service? That is, why isn't discipleship "making" a more frequent and positive response, on our part, to life's call? Obviously deterrents to religious ritual or activity are culturally manifold. However, at another level, the Word falls on hard ground due to a person having no constant object in the sense of "object relations," that internal psychic structure that should have been laid down in early years of human development. Psychic structure is built according to self-psychology by the internalization of validation and value from outside the very young person. Technically, individuals get sufficient mirroring through transference to build the primitive ego. Primarily, the growing child carries along his or her little psychic part that is secure in one's worth regardless of whatever else is going on. Sometimes that object becomes obscured or distorted, if it exists in the first place, by substance abuse, neglect, or trauma. Under those conditions the primitive self has to be re-parented through the Gospel story, rehabilitation, Alcoholics Anonymous (AA), and other supportive measures. The idea is that the concept of a higher power renews and revitalizes the process of object relations by reinstituting validation and worth.

Whatever the level or content of God talk, one is thrown back onto the groundbreaking work of Rizzuto.[7] She is among the first to suggest a resonance between a healthy psychic structure and spiritual symbols. Further, Sorenson, building on Rizzuto and "attachment theory," records that research suggests "adults with secure attachments (between parent and child) were likely to envision God as loving and accessible. By contrast, adults who were classified as having an avoidant attachment style were most likely to describe themselves as agnostics or atheists."[8]

Most of us who have chosen to follow Jesus find, in him, an objective, historical object capable of providing the loving care that conjoins and reflects the internal reality that the individual develops while learning to walk. Historically, for each of us, relationships within the earliest years "fuzz out" and get lost to memory. But generally, a healthy person can come back to a faith in God

---

7. Rizzuto, *The Birth of the Living God*, 90.
8. Sorenson, *Minding Spirituality*, 108.

through Christ because they have the sensors to recognize the abstract symbols at a subconscious level. So the saga is about returning to a language about one's validation, the feeling that one is secure in it and good fruits issue forth from it. The rehabilitative work of counselors, therapists, and their supervisors focus on the re-parenting, the re-validation of the individual (of psychic parts) and thus re-mirror the worth and acceptance of the client involved. In sum, there is stony ground on which the Gospel will fall. Yet God is at work in their lives.

It is generally agreed that people experience reality in events. Learning anew, hearing the Gospel story again, takes place through participation in activities. These events open up the personality configuration to the care of the neighbor and the rejuvenation of the Holy Spirit. In events occurring through the ministries of the church, one finds significant potential for both evangelization and education. Meaningful events are aligned with the hurts and needs of those around us. Churches have begun to offer mission programs which model ways to be available to the neighbor in need. Some also offer, along with AA, programs such as Celebrate Recovery where supportive groups minister to various other disorders or issues.

Our worth and growth must begin in relationship with at least one parenting person. Likewise, spiritual renewal may be expected from person-to-person relationships. Personal evangelism could best be described through the demonstration of Christlike care for the nearest neighbor. As prospective believers review discipleship in others, they not only look for a story of Jesus, but also seek to experience how this story is being lived out in the here and now, in the real world of postmodern times. Thankfully there are living examples of disciples who care like he cared, sacrificed in like manner of love, and served as he modeled to serve. And by God's grace through the power of the Holy Spirit, the Gospel message is heard anew, accepted, and lived. The ultimate expert on the topic of discipleship must surely be Dietrich Bonhoeffer. He comments at one place:

> As Christ bears our burdens, so ought we to bear the burdens of our fellow-men. . . . My brother's burden which I

must bear is not only his outward lot, his natural characteristics and gifts, but quite literally his sin. And the only way to bear that sin is by forgiving it. Forgiveness is the Christlike suffering which is the Christian's duty to bear.
... Suffering, then, is the badge of true discipleship.[9]

Discipleship is possible because of the prevenient work of the Holy Spirit utilizing our natural and learned capacities to respond and care for self and others. The sacramental life of the church is also the bedrock of our discipleship.

The Eucharist, in many ways, suggests that we are all transgressors, even as the Lord's Prayer has prepared us to understand. But further it places before us a vast cosmos of forgiveness, against which we may realign and review our various transgressions. We find there some restitution before we can restore things with others. Thereafter, we look across the table and are commanded to forgive the brother, sister, and neighbor. We dare not forget that forgiveness is a halfway house toward renewal and change for one's lifestyle. Forgiveness is something one does not do so much for the offender, although that is the goal. It is necessary ultimately for healing within the victim. Forgiveness breaks up the power cycle, taking back at least the dignity of halting the self-perpetuating violence in one's soul. This is not an attribution of guilt upon the self; it is a proactive stance and statement that the victim transcends being the mere thing upon which some cruel act was committed; transcendence is the soul's work, the spiritual journey anyone must take toward healing.

For the Christian disciple, a new vision is seen and new horizon offered to others. There is a wholeness in ordinary people that even professional "helpers" may ignore, that even a victim may choose to see. This revision of a fellow human being, one loved and forgiven by God, opens extraordinary possibilities to both perpetrator or victim. This option cannot be accounted for any other way than through the entry of the grace of Christian love. Through Christ, forgiveness came into the world. Only through his strength and spirit does one move beyond the natural urges for retribution

---

9. Bonhoeffer, *The Cost of Discipleship*, 100.

in order to reconcile with an offending neighbor. We are led by the prayer: "Forgive us our trespasses as we forgive those who trespass against us."

Isn't it possible that, at some level, Barb has trespassed against herself, against her own best interests and those of others? Working with her involved a measure of confirmation for her urgent impulse to reconnect (see Integrity, p. 15). She does not converse in those terms, but a nudge arising from some corner of awareness is moving her as a glacier pushing down a long valley. In Barb's case, was it anxiety that brought her into therapy? More likely it was her sense of isolation connected with a longing for deeper connection, a broken branch of her integrity. That yearning is a preparation for the ministry of the Holy Spirit. The Spirit's work is the reunion of our fragments of personhood along with communion shared with others.

A last chat with Barb is recorded here:

Counselor: It has been a while. What have you been up to?

Barb: Not as much as I really want. The time drags, and I've been thinking. . . .

Counselor: That's a great beginning . . . thinking about what?

Barb: I have been thinking about Sarah. She lived in the same housing with me before I left Sacramento.

Counselor: And what about her?

Barb: Sarah was lonely like me. We would run into each other in the hallway. Got acquainted that way. So sometime we'd play a game of hearts or something. Once I got sick. Since she didn't see me for several days, she came looking. When she found out I hadn't eaten, here came the soup and stuff. I dreamed of Sarah the other night, and she is still on my mind. As a matter of fact, I'm going back to Sacramento and look her up.

Counselor: My, it must have been a powerful dream. What can you tell me about it?

Barb: It was just . . . kind of a feeling, really . . . where I thought of Sarah.

Reflections on Spirituality in Pastoral Psychotherapy

> Counselor: She came back to mind. Recalled the nice things she did. Really, you think one good turn deserves another.... Is that it?
>
> Barb: Not exactly—I'm really wondering about that old rundown hotel. Wondering if she is making it all by herself—maybe sick, hungry. I am thinking that I have the time. She might need me. Something tells me I ought to go and find her. Could be I still need her. I need someone to look after and someone to look after me.
>
> Counselor: Your willingness to find her and support her seems very thoughtful and generous. Have you ever wondered where this concern originates? Where it comes from?
>
> Barb: Well, as I say, I had this dream. What else could it be?
>
> Counselor: Mysteries and wonders seem to have a sacred edge.
>
> Barb: You mean there is something holy about caring?
>
> Counselor: Barb, in my view, a cup of water offered to a thirsty person is a gift of power and love. So might be said of a journey in kindness and care.
>
> Barb: Not sure of any of that, it just seems to be the time. Something I have to do. I've appreciated getting to know you; I'm leaving on Saturday. Thanks again.

Barb was responding to kindness, offered by a "little old lady" in her former living quarters. That kindness, perhaps in some word or act, had lingered in her memory awaiting to resurface when someone, or some experience, called attention to a similar or parallel event. Barb was not overtly responding to a call of Christ, nor was she a candidate for church membership. There can be, however, a more general fullness in humankind wherein God is at work in quiet corners with no fanfare whatsoever. God doesn't wait for his "official" disciples, although they are essential too, to go about recreating a loving place—in a rundown abode in Sacramento.

Unlike Barb's return, Melissa had to go home by another route. Melissa's renewal began with an unusual kindness toward herself, one that extended beyond immediate gratification to beginning life over on other terms. That, also, may be seen as a gracious gift of God awaiting to be called by its proper name. Bonhoeffer's famous quip, "when Christ calls, he calls you to come and die,"[10] certainly applies—beginning with one's own self-denial so that hope and wholeness can take over.

Prayers and travel mercies are offered for you Barb, Melissa, and everyone as well. Discipleship begins with a turn in the road, a stop sign, a refreshing oasis, and a map for life.

---

10. Bonhoeffer, *The Cost of Discipleship*, 99.

10

Longing

Dale admitted to being suicidal. He had a plan and was serious about carrying it out. He stepped out in front of a moving car. The driver swerved, but his arm was hit. He didn't succeed at suicide that time, although he sustained an injured arm. He was talked into a cab and sent to the ER for assessment. That figures into his present condition. The ER admission notes, along with the arm, suggest he has other injuries as well. Dale is truly one of the most memorable, heart-wrenching cases of pure pathos and tragedy seen in some time. These are notes from some months ago.

The story unfolding with Dale is a tragic one: on the one hand, the enduring fact of parental love; and on the other, resistance to change. Parental "longing" endures.

Phone calls continue from Gil (Dale's father) about Dale, either to brief me or complain about him. Dale is a drug addict, dealer, and generally chaotic in every way. The *Diagnostic and Statistical Manual of Mental Disorders 5* (DSM-5) would classify him as an antisocial personality disorder, given his history of floridly acting out since his early teens. This family has been subjected to Dale's various shenanigans for over thirty years. After having only one child, the couple chose to adopt Dale when he was under a year old. They struggled keeping him in school and out of trouble for most of his early years. Gil and Carrie have disengaged with him off and on over his adulthood. He shows up to be taken in, from time

Longing

to time, when he is down and out. Lately they cast him off once and for all, they say, having agreed to his macabre contract that for a thousand dollars he would drop out of their lives forever. For a while he has made good on the deal. Some honor among thieves! Some say the parents should have shoved him off years ago. Now in their senior years they yearn; they long for rest.

Lately Gil and Carrie appeared at my doorstep for some sense of resolution and peace. Gil declares upon arrival, "We have been set up. I hope he neither calls nor shows up at my house ever again!" Well, they are coming in as a family, with Dale, today. It weighs heavily on this therapist on how to find the wisdom and strength to get them through this. The dilemma is formidable. It is crystal clear that Dale has run out of resources, pain management, and self-respect. He is on the verge of gang membership (again) and criminal behavior. Is that better than wasting away alone, hungry, and in pain? On the other hand, Gil and Carrie are at their wits' end. How does that help? And in this situation, what in fact is help?

Following the last session, an emergency call came in yesterday that Dale was threatening to provoke the police to come in and kill him. He was being evicted from his apartment on Friday afternoon. I listened intently during Carrie's near-hysterical phone call. Given that the man is in such dire straits, should they consider going to him? When Gil returned home in the afternoon, they decided not to intervene since Carrie had notified the police about the situation. The sheer helplessness is profound and overreaching when it comes to the management of this fellow whose incapacities are so absurd and ubiquitous. He is resistant to help and yet so helpless; parents feel so exploited, spent. What to do with a forty-year-old child who hasn't the grace to receive grace? The object there is to find a way for everyone to win; so far everyone has lost.

Any family therapist engaged with this family must juggle a multitude of issues. The multiple dimensions include the specifics of how to manage Dale's mental and social condition, how to support two aging parents, and how to support the family connection to the degree that it is possible. Beyond the consultative arrangements dealing with his social work and psychiatric services, individual counseling with Dale focused on addressing his pervading depression. Suggestions and confrontations are required to assist him in making the best choices vis-a-vis those who entice him back into destructive lifestyles. The nagging and most challenging choices for the therapist involved the parents' care and continuing support for Dale, their son, for their own security and sanity. In a nutshell, should the parents emotionally "un-adopt" this person who has caused them untold misery over the years? It is not acceptable and sufficient for a pastoral counselor to sit by passively, reflecting on the client's moods and wishes. In order to move beyond empathy, pastoral psychotherapy involves an intelligent and informed confrontation providing options for them beyond the levels of their insight and inclinations. The following discussion explores the issues that are background for such a confrontation.

Gil and Carrie want fervently to do the best thing for Dale. They are tempted, as most parents, to fall into the knee-jerk compliance of bailing out the kids, persisting in allowing them to self-destruct even after tough love's gallant efforts. The problem with a lot of offspring—and adults—who have severe mental disorders is that they take and take without ever having the facility to self-correct, that being the lasting prayer and hope of parents and helping professionals. Until some authoritative benchmark is discovered and observed, exploitive behavior may persist. Pastoral counseling avoids direction and preachment. It should be, however, prepared with explanations of Christian principles. To what degree does Christian ethics require sacrificial love? A brief review of Christian ethics is prompted by the question.

Augustine clearly lays out the ethical foundations that are built upon by Aquinas, and the modern edifice of Christian doctrine and behavior. In "On Christian Doctrine," he asserts the biblical tenet that one should love God and one's neighbor as himself. Having established that no one should deny self-love, he should love all neighbors equally. However, since that is impossible, given our temporal conditions, one loves those closest to one's attention and affection.[1] "The moral issue of ordering loyalties to biological family members, church community, and all humanity remains

---

1. Augustine, "On Christian Doctrine," 631.

Longing

central to Christian ethics and to all moral thought."[2] "Western moral theological thought on the *ordo amoris* (order of love) has always required a leaning toward the neediest that counters familial insularity or overindulgence of the nearest."[3] And as Pope has commented: "Despite many exceptions, as Aquinas noted, ties of blood seem to be strongest and most durable of bonds, and it does seem to be the case . . . that 'altruism appears to be substantially hard-core when directed at closest relatives.'"[4] In a recent review of Roman Catholic ethics, Pope reviews a recent article penned by Karl Rahner. The general thesis is that:

> Whenever a genuine love of man attains its proper nature and its moral absoluteness and depth, it is in addition always so underpinned and heightened by God's saving grace that it is also love of God, whether it be explicitly considered to be such love by the subject or not.[5]

Reflecting further on Catholic precedents, Pope underscores the *caritas* position with appeals to the great doctor of the church.

> Thomas was of course well aware of Luke 14:26 and similar passages, and interprets them as requiring, not an abolition of love of family and self simpliciter, but rather their false and improper counterfeits. Whereas caritas subordinates love of self to love for God, cupiditas reverses the order. Charity by implication respects a parallel distinction between ordered and disordered kin loyalties. Just as improper love of self in fact amounts to "hatred," so by implication, disordered love of family entails a de facto "hatred of family."[6]

---

2. Post, *Unlimited Love*, 124.

3. Post, *Unlimited Love*, 123.

4. Pope, "The Order of Love and Recent Catholic Ethics: A Constructive Proposal," 275.

5. Pope, "The Order of Love and Recent Catholic Ethics: A Constructive Proposal," 257.

6. Pope, "The Order of Love and Recent Catholic Ethics: A Constructive Proposal," 263.

Reflections on Spirituality in Pastoral Psychotherapy

Through these passages, Pope has identified man's self-love as a form of hatred, and a parallel to that is the "hatred" involved in disordered family love. It could be well agreed that the convoluted "love" which looks more like "hatred" doesn't square well with Rahner's own position, viz that all human love is in some fashion undergirded by God's love.

From the Protestant perspective, other options appear. Williams summarizes and then comments on Reinhold Niebuhr's perspective on love and self-sacrifice in the following way:

> ... sacrificial love, the agape of the Gospel, must transcend mutual love. Agape is given freely for the sake of the other and is heedless of reward or response. Only agape leads to fulfillment, but the fulfillment must be the unintended result; otherwise love masks our self-seeking and then the goal is lost. Niebuhr argues that sacrificial love is the "impossible possibility"; he has exposed in a masterly way the sin in our pretenses of morality and brotherhood. It is grace alone, with the forgiveness it holds, which can release us to recognize and in some fragmentary way begin to live in self-giving love for God and neighbor.[7]

That is, whether in a family context or in social settings at large, love—even that which qualifies as close to *agape* as humans can muster—falls short. It must be completed by God's gift of grace alone. One might think of people, following the Christ event, who have given their lives for noble and worthy causes. Thomas More, Dietrich Bonhoeffer, Martin Luther King Jr.—all come to mind but no one of the above set out to be self-sacrificing. Sacrifice chose them as a matter of principle. Each stood on the ground of his best light and love. For Niebuhr, nonetheless, their best efforts, unrewarded sacrifice, reached their *telos* only in God's providential care.

Discussing ethics in his volume on contemporary psychologies, Don Browning cites such notables as Outka and Janssens who have synthesized a range of ethical theory.[8] Browning notes that they have successfully followed Augustine's program of Christian

---

7. Williams, *The Spirit and the Forms of Love*, 193.
8. Browning, *Religious Thought and the Modern Psychologies*, 146f.

Longing

ethics, having joined *eros* and *agape* by placing self-sacrificial behavior at the service of mutual service, respect, and justice. *Caritas* (charity) implies that one need not and should not self-objectify by allowing another's exploitive behavior. Following this train of thought, one is led to offer his best gift of love at a crucial juncture with the prayer that the gift may shift the course of community. This gift is a penultimate act intended to reestablish mutuality in a relationship gone wrong. "Mutuality and equal-regard are the ideal, and sacrificial love is derived from them."[9] Williams moves the prospect further by suggesting that self-denial and sacrifice prepare for the claim of and love of God upon an event, thus engendering hope for self-fulfillment and completion in God's Kingdom.[10] That is, God bequeaths his forgiving *agape* at the boundaries of human existence or in the abyss of despair as a creative and reconstitutive influence on life.

Victims of exploitation, whether physical, emotional, or financial are left—at least up to this point—with the Christian ethical options as follows:

One may follow a track with Niebuhr, where self-sacrifice is the greatest ideal of Christian love and self-fulfillment, but fails the best of human efforts. Thus God's grace is attributed to those who seek it. Niebuhr seems to strike out on the hard-playing field of reality.

Or one may choose to love in a sacrificial way toward the goal of reestablishing mutual respect and regard, according to Janssens. The implication is that once offered, without attaining such mutuality, further acts of love may not be forthcoming. There is a lot of appeal here; however, most serious offenders and/or perpetrators don't play fair.

Or one loves sacrificially as a token offering for which God alone can bring meaning and fulfillment—gifts given in preparation for God's embedded *agape*, an activity proposed and described by Williams. In many ways, Williams has grasp on a grain of truth.

---

9. Browning, *Religious Thought and the Modern Psychologies*, 152.
10. Williams, *The Spirit and the Forms of Love*, 210.

Responsible Christians' acts of love, even with the very finest offerings, come to completion only in the ultimate *agape* of God.

These have been the options to this point in the discussion. However, and finally, another voice is heard. Miroslav Volf, a native of Croatia, writes out of his own firsthand experience of teaching in Croatia during the war in the former Yugoslavia. He says at one point while discussing justice between adversaries:

> . . . reconciliation is ultimately possible only through injustice being forgiven and, finally, forgotten. The act of forgiveness will name injustice as injustice and therefore demand that its causes be removed; the act of forgetting will be possible only after the threat of repeated violation has disappeared. . . . Is wrath against injustice appropriate? Yes! Must the perpetrator be restrained? By all means! Is punishment for the violation necessary? Probably. But all these indispensable actions against the unjust must be situated in the framework of the will to embrace the unjust. For only our mutual embrace within the embrace of the triune God can we find redemption and experience perfect peace.[11]

In sum, Volf has opened another pathway for reconciliation between Dale and his weary parents. It involves the choices of the parents who wish to maintain contact with their son (i.e., have the will to embrace him, even though his past behaviors have been painful and destructive). Hypothetically, given Dale's options to reject his former lifestyle and embark on a more responsible one, reunion is within reach. Volf is on target to suggest that forgiveness and reunion hangs in the balance of whether "the threat of repeated violation has disappeared." Forgiveness is, then, offered and finally misdeeds forgotten. Reconciliation begins, according to Volf, with the willingness to accept, even embrace, the perpetrator—whoever and whatever his prior deeds—given that form of justice that includes punishment and change. Volf is able to echo in no small measure the profound parable of Jesus known as the "Prodigal Son"[12] *because*, as it is implied, the younger son repented,

11. Volf, *Exclusion and Embrace*, 224.
12. Luke 15:11. See Nouwen, *The Return of the Prodigal Son*.

accepted the "medicine" of tending a pigpen, and chose to change his behavior.

With the summary review of ethical literature, we return to the case of Gil, Carrie, and Dale. The challenge for the therapist in addressing the issues with Dale regards the existential matter of Trust (see p. 15). An Axis II[13] (DSM-5) individual, by definition, tends to avoid the therapeutic alliance on which remediation can occur. Thus engaging and holding were offered to Dale without much visible result. Supportive work with Gil and Carrie was more hopeful. Although they sought relief from the perpetual distress, they stubbornly refused to cast their son aside. Volf encourages Christians to maintain relationships with offenders—even perpetrators of crime—as the signal that human restitution is possible, and ultimately, through forgiveness, pain and suffering may be forgotten. Given the words and wisdom of the best of sages, it remains for each believer in Christ to make a choice on how and in what form shall love be shaped.

This conversation occurred with Carrie and Gil:

> Counselor: I know this has been a trying time for you, Carrie.
>
> Carrie: Well, it is even worse when Dale can't function by himself in his apartment. Then he comes out to stay with us. He is up all night watching TV and smoking. I hate it.
>
> Counselor: Yeah, you guys have been really longsuffering with Dale. When he comes to visit, wouldn't that be a good time to set guidelines for him?
>
> Carrie: Oh, that would just start a fight. I am so weary. Of course, this is nothing new. His father and I have struggled with him since he was a little kid. He was always in trouble either with the law or at school.
>
> Counselor: Seems like more of the same. More time. More patience. More caring.
>
> Carrie: I know his back must be painful, and that is just the beginning of all his problems.

13. See Multiaxial Assessment for personality disorders, DSM-5.

Counselor: What do you and Gil say to each other to keep on supporting the guy?

Carrie: We say he is our son. What else can we say?

Counselor: You aren't giving up on him, are you? You seem to stand together through thick and thin. Seems you guys are in agreement, of same mind to keep giving and hurting.

Carrie: Over our morning devotions we plan the day and pray for strength and hope. And you know, Gil is getting much better at leading in prayer. I am amazed how he pours out his heart to God. And, of course, I get to overhear. We both ask for guidance and help to deal with his illness, his foul mouth, and vulgar outlook.

Counselor: And part of that guidance is for you. As I suggested earlier, your fondest hopes for him prevail as a parent. However, parents don't condone unloving behavior—since that usually results in unloving and hurtful actions. And I am sure your prayers are answered as God works in our midst. My prayers for you is that you two will be kinder, more loving to yourselves.

Gil: What do you mean, more loving and caring for ourselves? We're really doing our best!

Counselor: I'm suggesting that when he takes advantage of your kind heart, your heart is hurting. He is getting his way at your expense.

Gil: We've been hurting a long time . . . that's for sure.

Carrie: Yes, we turned him over to the Lord a long time ago. Now, it seems all we can do is turn ourselves, as well, over to God.

Counselor: I believe my job is to help you explore ways to reduce being stung by his habits, and I think God is at work in this with us. Wouldn't you like to do that?

Carrie: Well, of course, you know we would.

Over the lengthy period of contact with Dale and his parents, it became apparent that Gil and Carrie would never abandon their son. They continued "arm's length" contact, and worked for his decent housing and physical rehabilitation. They are suspected of providing money when the SSI got fouled up. Over the course of time, there was little change in the basic orientation that Dale had toward life, with this one exception: he gained enough self-respect to see and talk about the goal of autonomy. Old habits worked against him. More emotional distance seemed appropriate for this loving couple. Parental love can and does forgive. In Dale's case, however, it was really hard to forgive and forget. Truly one can claim that their sacrifices have been squandered in the pathos of the human condition. On the other hand, they never ceased to love their son or to pray in his behalf. In many ways parental love cannot be extinguished. Neither should it be eclipsed by the failure to love, at least on an equal basis, oneself.

11

Hope

It was Wednesday afternoon in our intensive outpatient clinic. A group of girls ranging in age from thirteen to eighteen sat around the room bragging about their various suicide attempts. One claimed that if someone was really serious about death, she wouldn't "fail" at it. She would find a way to succeed at death. Others countered that even with the intentionality and lethal equipment, it was still quite possible that life would persist. What a weird and bizarre discussion to be in progress among a quartet of kids! A sub-theme had to do with the question, what is on the other side of death? One petite sixteen-year-old was convinced there was simply blackness and nothing prevailed—and she was glad! She simply wanted to disappear: not to think, see, hear, or be. So disillusioned with life was she that the best thing to imagine was simply not to be. Her scratching, cutting, and other self-mutilation were emblems of her self-loathing and the disdain she held for everyone and everything that life had to offer.

Teenagers are naturally filled with "hope"; that is, unless prospects are dimmed due to pain and loss. Faithful counselors continue to anticipate the inbreaking of the eternal now.

The girls danced on the edge of, and could have wrestled with, the classic question: "Will I go to hell if I commit suicide?" This issue can easily throw the religious professional off guard and into

Hope

a quandary. On the one hand, a counselor or pastor does not want to encourage someone's suicide. On the other, the matter of hell depends on the questioner's expectation. Behind the question usually lie two quite poignant issues: (1) the individual is desperate and has become hopeless with his condition, and (2) the individual believes her past lifestyle has become a cumulative hell and assumes she/he has earned nothing but grief ahead.

Practitioners in pastoral care will bring assurance that nothing done in life deserves eternal hell. God views each person as a child in need, a child who is loved and offered life now and life everlasting. A pastoral counselor should have two ready resources: a sound eschatology and the pastoral skill to address the ultimacy issues of the flock. From these youngsters' queries about death and suicide, the matters of heaven and hell, emerges the need to address the outlines of an eschatology. What is expected beyond the temporal stage upon which we now live? The pastoral task, as always, is to listen to the experiences of the world, and respond in faith. In this instance, what do people say about their own views, premonitions, fears? And what is our response to be?

I begin with three entries which appeared in my chaplain's casebook. Each suggests the inherent "nearness of another realm" beyond this temporal one that I was called upon to consider.

Note 1: Some years ago a *Guideposts* article written by Catherine Marshall was entitled "A Glimpse of Eternity." She tells the story of Betty Malz who returned literally from the dead enriched with a unique, glowing spiritual experience. A coma had enveloped her for weeks. The doctors had pronounced complete expiration. Twenty minutes later she sat up, removed the sheet, and ordered a meal. These events are sparse, or at least sparsely reported. Nonetheless, as with time, a suggestion exists regarding a mystical convergence of death with afterlife. And for Betty, there was a moment when the world of spirit and this world of time and space fused together. Her report, like others, supports the hope that the human spirit will eventually metamorphose into some new creation proclaimed in the Scripture.

Note 2: Two individuals in an AA group described their experiences while suffering a severe illness. Each witness felt the presence of an afterlife and new environment. One person commented on her experience of being led down a road that separated on one side into what appeared to be a happy and heavenly place, filled with light. On the other side was a putrid place, foul smelling with sounds of shrieks and groans. She was being led by a hooded and shrouded figure. Never, however, was she given or taken to a point of choice, just the awesome revelation of the two realms. How amazing it is that human beings are hardwired to be conscious of these realities, disclosed when the frontal lobe is basically out of commission. What do drug addicts know about theology or spirituality? Evidently a good deal. It would be plausibly apparent, if it made some concrete difference in their lifestyle and the choices of being in this world.

Note 3: Visit with Mrs. Greer this morning: she says she had always yearned to see Jesus, to know what he was really like, how he looked, sounded, taught. Now the patient lay quietly, save for the rattling in the chest. Doctors had done all they could for her and suggested that the family should be called. Immediately, her spouse quickly assembled the son from Albuquerque and the daughter from Albany. She continued to struggle for precious breath. Some hours passed. The family members arrived, and they assembled around her bed, pressing her hand gently with the caresses of care. Her eyes opened, and with halting words, gasping to breathe, she thanked each in turn, and gave thanks to God for their tender care. Her last words posed a question: "I know all my loved ones are here, but who is that in the corner?"

And lately, Dr. Eben Alexander has written up his coma-induced experience of wandering the netherland beyond life/death into a place where he ultimately came into communion with his long lost, long dead sister![1] It is truly an exciting exposition following a severe encounter with bacterial meningitis. Eben's work adds to the growing literature in the "beyond death experiences" genre.

So there are hints of eternity all around us. For some a touch of intuition will do; only a billboard will be noticed by others. This

---

1. Alexander, *Proof of Heaven*.

Hope

envelope of temporality is not all that it appears or presents itself to be. There is vastness in God's creative wonders: perhaps parallel universes, or multiverses. Science continues to probe the outer reaches of our known universe, all the while diminishing the significance of the short while we spend on this speck of sand, our Earth. Stephen Hawking comments that God cannot exist, based on his studies of black holes where time does not exist.[2] If there is no time, he surmises, then there could be no eternity and thus no place for God to be. He presupposes, I assume, that God is a temporal entity and requires a place to stand! For the rest of us, there are bridge moments, opportunities to touch the fringes of eternity.

In the face of much of the doom and gloom of our time, the church proclaims an Easter faith that involves God's own, persistent stewardship. The good Shepherd always finds the strays. The good Housekeeper always finds the lost coin. The good Father eternally seeks and receives the errant son. Likewise in all of God's creation, neither mass nor energy gets lost; it simply changes form and fashion. Since God "truly don't make no junk," God always rebuilds from the stubborn stuff of life, death, and hereafter. One could claim that the office of the Holy Spirit is the driver for the ever-constant renewal of the universe. That is a seedbed of hope. In other words, from the death of this temporal form, there is a grounding for an ultimate renewal in the eternal one. The eternal Spirit is constantly wooing human response to rejoice in the very fact of life itself, giving each person the latitude of what he or she will make of the gift. God never ceased to shepherd and watch over the Son Jesus and the events following his death.

The miracle of Easter is not comprehended by the historical events at the tomb that morning outside Jerusalem, as it is found in the fellowship of joy that surrounded the forthtelling. Mary's proclamation of the story to the frightened and fleeing disciples is miraculous. Mary heralds the events to follow. Both Luke and John introduce the resurrected Jesus back into community, with both family and friends. The disciples who are to become apostles become the primitive church. The fact that a people called "church"

---

2. Hawking, *Into the Universe with Stephen Hawking*.

has survived this two thousand years is an unfathomable mystery and wonder. At the end of the day, the Easter message is one of connection and belonging. As Jesus belonged to the Father, as Christ is the Bride of the church, we have the grand privilege to honor and celebrate our communion. On this topic the late Charles Schultz was an apostle. Snoopy's activities in the Peanuts cartoon come to mind: Easter is about distributing colored eggs of happiness and joy to all unexpected and undeserving people and places. When really on track, the church is the "Snoopy" of the world, distributing the eggs of joy to all who have "eyes to see and ears to hear." The joy is all about Christ's connection with the eternal Father, who never lets go, and our fellowship with them. We are bound together in joy! Now the challenge is to feel, celebrate, and show this joy to a world of doom and gloom. One of the pastor's privileges is to represent, symbolize, and on occasion articulate this joy in the clinic or the counseling room.

The joy of the church's faith is not based on sporadic anecdotes or narrations of the mysteries of the afterlife, nor scientific discoveries, as interesting as they are. Joy, as we know it, arises from the church's faith arising across the centuries and the steadfast hope for eternity. According to Pannenberg's eschatology, God views the present and the end things all together, without distinction. The consummation of all time is eternally present, and God interjects it into the flow of contemporary occurrences.[3] This portends that, at least in God's view, the present realities of the perfected person and the perfected Kingdom are available to us through Christ, past and present.

Holiness has partly to do with capturing the moment (*kairos*), truly seeing from a Kingdom perspective, as if it were the fulfillment of all things, and responding to the moment according to that glory, rather than whatever outer shell is being presented "at the time." Therefore, there is a constant "inbreaking" of the future into the present. People focus chiefly on the piecework chores directly ahead. Rather, the future is arriving within God's gifts of insight into consciousness. In a similar vein, these thoughts appear

---

3. Pannenberg, *Systematic Theology III*, 606f.

complimentary to Whitehead's view of process.[4] Each moment "prehends" the prior moment as God provides the maximum fulfillment among the latent choices and opens the future. So the past has been solidified into eternity, sealed in some sense. What is behind us cannot be changed according to historical fact; what can be changed is what one remembers and reframes for the choices in the present—and prestages the future.

Sometimes eternity flashes into our consciousness like glimmering meteor showers. These arrive in critical moments, decisions that can bend history whether for one person or a community. As the hymn extols: "once to every man and nation comes a moment to decide." I call these Gethsemane events, moments where the future hangs in the balance. It is a time to pray: "Lead us not into temptation, and deliver us from evil," or deliver us from pain. I sense that suicidal patients have just such moments, where the future hangs in the balance and they decide to "opt out" of being around in the future moments. In a cinematic presentation some years back, *A Man for All Seasons*, Thomas More is portrayed as a man with a Catholic conscience in the face of Henry VIII's licentiousness. He paid the ultimate price, as did Bonhoeffer and King in our own time. The prospect and processes of holy living and holy dying were held close to the heart of John Wesley. He was one who was able to grasp certain moments, perhaps an inbreaking—*kairos*—of an imperceptible moment when someone has the good judgment to take the courage step. More and Wesley, each in his own way, were able to bend history in the direction of the better—whatever that historical context might be. Wesley had much to teach based on the patristics of the early church, and we are still grounded as he was in the crucible of Cappadocian professions on sanctification. It seems that this fits well with the whole concept that critical moments come our way, and they have the power to bend history forever.

At last everyone has to take a risk about the future. The challenge may appear on any daily basis at the most expected moment. Commuting from work one day, intoned over the radio came the familiar lyrics of an old hymn: "We'll Meet Again Some Sweet Day."

---

4. Brown, et al., *Process Philosophy and Christian Thought*, 219.

Reflections on Spirituality in Pastoral Psychotherapy

It prompted a quaint thought. Could it really be that one receives what he or she prays for—given that each human being is given the radical freedom to do with life according to the raw materials at hand, each born with the freedom of individual choice? That principle, radically applied as faith, could also include and extend well beyond this physical life. I have come to suspect that whatever someone expects (i.e., faith forward) based on the experiences and choices of earthly life, one will in fact receive. Whatever he dreams of, prays for, lives for is finally formulated in this life or the next. God, the Giver of all good gifts, allows each person to design the afterlife he chooses: expect nothing/, receive nothing; expect completion and reunion, receive heaven. Eternity is entirely in human hands. Eternity is now. Perhaps this is another way of restating what St. Paul proposes in his Corinthian correspondence (1 Corinthians 15:25) except in an agrarian motif, viz that as a seed is planted it shall sprout in kind. We plant this earthly existence and God reclothes it with fitting apparel for eternity.

In this section we have attempted to listen to several sources of human experience. From the public domain, one source is people's reports of intuitions of a trans-temporal realm. These events escape complete definition; one cannot discern shape, size, or possibility. The church of Jesus Christ claims that we worship a God who never gives up on us and all creation. The prevailing symbol of that is the resurrection of Jesus and the subsequent historical community of faith. The church's best minds have extrapolated on the continuity of God's care, both now and eternally, without the necessity to provide the details of what awaits sentient beings. Some may subscribe to "Pascal's wager"[5]—i.e., he or she becomes a gambler. Either one bets on the meaning and contours of a life of love after the manner of Jesus or, with Hawking,[6] is willing to make the best of what these days bring and expect nothing more.

As a symbol of the church's faith, the chaplain met that day with a tiny clique full of gloom. His task was to listen and hear the pain as the young women described their despair. He refused to

---

5. See plato.stanford.edu/entries/pascal-wager.
6. Hawking, *A Brief History of Time*, 140f.

Hope

"buy in" to their "hell," and instead confirmed their innate value and worth. I believe this is "earnest money" on eternity. Their conversation is rife with the dynamics of both *anxiety* and *mobility* (see p. 15), far, to be sure, from any secure trust in a future life.

Let's listen in on the chat with the girls:

> Ann: I found my pills in my mother's medicine cabinet. It was easy.
>
> Judy: That does sound easy, but since I scratch myself anyway, why not just go ahead and cut the arm vein?
>
> Alex: I think you both are just jerking us around. If you were serious about offing yourself, you'd have found a way—and done it.
>
> Ann: Don't give me that; I enjoyed just sort of drifting away. The light dimmed, and I sort of just went to sleep. . . . That is, until some AH grabbed me and took me to the hospital and all that sh-t.
>
> Counselor: Sounds like you girls are discussing a pizza party. This is heavy stuff, thinking about death. You are not trash to be tossed into a dumpster.
>
> Alex: Well, we feel like trash and feel like sh-t most of the time, and nobody does anything about it or cares anything about it.
>
> Counselor: And what does care look like for you, Alex?
>
> Alex: I don't know. . . . Maybe just to start life all over again. . . .
>
> Counselor: To be born with a new start?
>
> Alex: New place, new home, new parents, new . . . EVERYTHING!
>
> Counselor: To whom do you go to get all that?
>
> Alex: I don't know where everything comes from; how can I know that?
>
> Counselor: A whole lot of stuff is born out of our decisions and choices. As life comes to us as a gift, we can either honor it or trash it.
>
> Alex: I'm a gift, alright! Like, for sure.

Reflections on Spirituality in Pastoral Psychotherapy

> Counselor: You know, some time ago, an adult thought you were their most precious and wonderful gift.
>
> Alex: Well, it didn't take long for my mother to get over that.
>
> Counselor: I have a faith that you still are pretty precious and wonderful.
>
> Alex: Faith in what?
>
> Counselor: I think God treats us all as pretty precious and wonderful.
>
> Ann: If God cared anything about us, he'd just turn out the lights and we could rest and get some peace—for God's sake.
>
> Judy: There's probably not any such thing as God anyway. There is just now, today, and this miserable hospital.
>
> Counselor: Maybe this hospital is where God lives. What we experience here could be a signal that God intends peace and joy and value for all of you.
>
> Ann: Well, this place is certainly better than wandering around in the streets, if you ask me.

For these young women of my spirituality group, there is the long road back to unlearning and reprogramming, that they could come to see themselves as precious, cherished, and embraced. That road will need frequent rest stops, where they can enjoy refuge and rest offered by empathy, presence, and trustworthiness. Refuge will be found in the reconnection with a community, Spirit filled with joy. There they may return to the wonder that is every child's birthright, rather than wandering the lonely streets of abandonment. Nothing they have done deserves the self-inflicted hell of cutting and purging derived from self-loathing born of horrendous experiences. Their demons make life a constant Halloween. Our pastoral prayer is that Origen of Alexandria (185–254) was right, that even the demons can be redeemed—some of them even in this life. He went on to claim, of course, that even the devils themselves will be saved into an afterlife with God.[7] While in prayer, I share this greeting sent to friends from another era:

---

7. Tillich, *A History of Christian Thought*, 64; Walker, *A History of the Christian Church*, 77.

Hope

There is nothing I can give you which you have not, but there is much, very much, that while I cannot give it, you can take.

No heaven can come to us unless our hearts find rest in it today. Take heaven! No peace lies in the future which is not hidden in this present instant. Take peace! The gloom of the world is but a shadow. Behind it, yet within reach, is joy. There is a radiance and glory in the darkness, could we but see, and to see we have only to look. I beseech you to look. Life is so generous a giver, but we, judging its gifts by their covering, cast them away as ugly or heavy or hard. Remove the covering, and you will find beneath it a living splendor, woven of love, by wisdom, with power.

Welcome it, grasp it, and you touch the angel's hand that brings it to you. Everything we call a trial, a sorrow, or a duty, believe me that angel's hand is there: the gift is there, and the wonder of an overshadowing presence. Our joys too; be as content with them as joys. They too, conceal diviner gifts.

And so, at this time, I greet you. Not quite as the world sends greetings, but with profound esteem and with the prayer that for you now and forever, the day breaks and the shadows flee away. (Fra. Giovanni, AD 151)

And so I left the group that day with this thought: Oh, you are so, so unaware, but as St. Mark phrased his insight, "the time is now full; the Kingdom is at hand."[8]

---

8. Mark 1:15.

12

Postscript

The claim may now be made that the Rubicon has been crossed. I have explored the theological materials that might have been elicited from a particular clinical challenge. There is a valid assertion that a bridge exists between Schleiermacher, who set the "liberal" assumptions and program in motion, in response to the Enlightenment reliance on romanticism and reason, and Kierkegaard who etched in stark relief the gulf between God's providential grace and man's sin.[1] That bridge has been constructed of many planks to be sure, notably the thought and work of William James, A. N. Whitehead, and the process theologians who followed. In specific ways we have departed from one of the theological titans of the twentieth century, Karl Barth. Early in his career, following Kierkegaard, Barth declared a resounding "No" to the culture religion of his day, as did Kierkegaard in his. The clear basis for Barth, seemingly, is also found in St. Paul: "I propose to preach one thing only and that is Christ, and him crucified" (1 Corinthians 2:2), and thereafter resurrected—speaking of a unified event of God. The case for St. Paul, the Reformers, and thereafter, Barth was to focus narrowly on the saving grace of God through the Christ

---

1. Regarding Barth: "Criticizing the Schleiermacher and Ritschl schools for their subjectivism and relativism, he put great emphasis on the otherness of God, the centrality of revelation, and the sinful nature of man." Walker, *A History of the Christian Church*, 544.

Postscript

event. *Sola fide*, by faith alone, was the normative code. There has been no interest here in glossing over the "cheap grace" and culture religion of the past or early decades of this century. There has been an honest search for credible ways to report God's disclosures and human appropriations. These issues form the context for effective and edifying counseling from a pastoral perspective.

So what does all this matter for the pastoral counselor? Counselors across the spectrum are now becoming more spiritually sensitive and aware, as Pargament[2] has adequately documented. His work has taken a major step toward disqualifying simplistic ideas about philosophical approaches, namely that either one depends on humanistic theories, or biblical quotations and injunctions injected into every situation. We find assistance also from N. T. Wright, who disclaims commonplace assumptions: "Either we see the world, and indeed ourselves, as full of signals of the presence of divinity, or we see the world empty of the divine, doing its own thing, with gods now far away. We become, in other words, either pantheists or dualists."[3] Perhaps as an afterthought or correction toward *panentheism*, Wright continues: "In ancient Judaism and early Christianity, heaven and earth, God's world and our world overlap and interlock..."[4]

At issue remain the notions of revelation and how they relate to an epistemology that makes sense in the contemporary venue. The matter put directly is: how does God disclose himself [*sic*] in ways that are perceptible to common folks? How does one apprehend the visitation of the sacred in people's lives, and how do they know it within a clinical setting with the help of pastoral counselors? My answer to this problem requires a sensitivity to the revelation in Christ as a unique event and a robust doctrine of the Holy Spirit. One's awareness of the Holy Spirit's reality cannot be left floating loftily in the atmosphere. The linkage between the sacred and celebration must have substance and take root in love. The love of God imparts and stimulates recharting one's future and

---

2. Pargament, *Spiritually Integrated Psychotherapy*.
3. Wright, *Simply Jesus*, 210.
4. Wright, *Simply Jesus*, 211.

empowers specific steps to reform one's relationships in the world. Again, revelation mediated by the Holy Spirit and epistemology make a dynamic duo.

The beginning place for a synthesis involves a revisit to Nicea (AD 325) and a review of the Trinity. The early fathers were hard pressed to establish that Jesus of Nazareth was truly the Son of God, the eternal *logos*, which set him apart from mere mortals. What appears to be lacking in the Nicene Creed is a full-fledged doctrine of the Holy Spirit,[5] which leaves us disquieted and bewildered regarding God's grace. The active work of God seen through the lenses of Whitehead and his followers provide muscle to the idea of the Holy Spirit. This provision empowers Wesley's doctrine of prevenient grace significantly and offers a path where God is disclosed and to which people may respond. That pathway is the God-given *agape*, a love so profound that it sparks a response, both from the head and the heart, from individuals who have sought connection and wholeness in themselves and relationally with their neighbors. Again, this requires the gift of the Holy Spirit to infuse our faith, which then empowers human love.

Through the work of a pastoral counselor, clients may ascertain that within their freedom they can choose a loving (respectful, or caring) response to themselves, their problems, and their relationships. The pastoral counselor acknowledges their response as a gift of God's immanent working of the Holy Spirit and may, in some conditions, call attention to the mystery (e.g., "where did that insight come from?"). Process theologians refer to God's immanence and propose that there is an immediate work in progress as human choices gather and sort God-given options—with the expectation that there is an unknown and unnamed urge toward that which is for every human being the optimal choice. This language and vision for reality opens the door to God's immediacy, beckon, and call.

A parallel process should become apparent. God loves his creatures extravagantly with the gifts of dizzying freedom, allowing them to choose their own course of life; so should the pastoral counselor and supervisor. The implication is that counselors are

---

5. Walker, *A History of the Christian Church*, 118.

Postscript

not coercive with their own ideas, goals, or prescriptions—not even with religious language. They bring their skills of forbearance, which allows clients to recognize their own salvation, whether in terms of healing or reconciliation. In this context, or posture, the client's work is seen as the visitation of the Spirit bestowing gifts beyond human craft or imagination.

What is the import of all of this theological discussion for the client who has walked off the street and settles uneasily in the chair across from the counselor? The client will assess whether the counselor he or she has chosen accesses the best of both the therapeutic and spiritual "tools" to address the issues at hand. Toward that end, competence in both areas has been the driving energy of this study. It has been assumed that the pastoral counselor has mastered his chosen therapeutic approach and rationale. For our purposes, four existential realities have been identified as the core issues to be addressed in any therapeutic venture: *anxiety*—the motivating dynamic that moves the person from crisis to counseling; *mobility*—the ability to explore the problems in their multiform aspects and to "unstick" from former paradigms of life; *integrity*—the search for internal and interpersonal reunion and wholeness; and finally, *trust*—the ability to make commitments to some value system that offers new life. These human functions have both psychological and spiritual components. The pastoral counselor will cherish and celebrate them both.

The concluding word is one about living in tension. It is the tension presented by the Trinitarian concept of God's loving intrapersonal relationship. We have wondered how to reconcile the efficacy of the Christ event with a contemporaneous experience of God's sacred presence and work. This issue surfaces in the corners of the counseling chamber and needs to be brought into the light of day. It is not done by quoting Scripture or doctrines of the church—at least not as such. The tension in sum is really a dialogue. The story of the Gospel event and the story of human experience ask probing and pertinent questions each to the other.

It is only done, further, by a context of love. Peck stated it so well in his conclusion that the best hope of helping others, even the evil ones, is through the methods of love.⁶ The pastoral counselor may be expert only in *phileo* with the anticipation of the Spirit's *agape*. As the case is made that we may never understand the events of Jesus of Nazareth without the disclosing love and work of the Spirit, neither shall we ever understand fully the immediate disclosure of the Spirit's gifts without a ready reference to the living and loving Christ.

As I began this project with a very personal word, it seems appropriate to close with one. It entails a memory of an evening when Edward C. Hobbs presented a program to college students during a Wesley Foundation meeting. That memory of Hobbs connects with the piece he penned as an introduction to a worship manual entitled *The Wesley Orders of Common Prayer*.⁷ He speaks there of one who has been mesmerized by the awesome revelation of Jesus Christ. Thereafter, he says, and I quote:

> It behooves me to cease my anxious care about my future, about the dangers which I fear might overwhelm me—and to offer all such concerns to him who cares for me—and who has assured us today of his care in all the Scripture we have heard.... Tomorrow, of course, I have forgotten that I can trust him, and that he cares for me; I am again attempting to live life on my terms, attempting to find security in the passing-ness of life, attempting to avoid the hands of One who gives both life and death, both Yes and No, both Cross and Resurrection. And as one who has forgotten, I am suddenly confronted by a Word which declares me to be a sinner, and calls me to repentance; and once more I am given his grace to enter another day—and so on, day after day. This is the story of my life.

Unfortunately one cannot—and should not—remain a sophomore all his life. One can, however, remain awestruck at the amazing grace given fresh every day, and this is the story of my life.

---

6. Peck, *People of the Lie*, 267.
7. Hobbs, *The Wesley Orders of Common Prayer*, 10.

Bibliography

Albom, Mitch. *Tuesdays with Morrie*. New York: Random House, 1997.
Alexander, Eben. *Proof of Heaven*. New York: Simon and Schuster, 2012.
American Psychiatric Association. *Diagnostic and Statistical Manual of Mental Disorders*. 5th ed. Arlington, VA: American Psychiatric Association, 2013.
Appelbaum, Stephen A. *Evocativeness*. Northvale, NJ: Jason Aronson, Inc., 2000.
Augustine. *On Christian Doctrine*. Great Books of the Western World 18. Chicago: University of Chicago Press, 1952.
Baron, Vida C. *The Aging Escape Zone*. First Books, 2000.
Barth, Karl. *Church Dogmatics I/2*. New York: Charles Scribner's Sons, 1956.
Beabout, Gregory R. "Kierkegaard on Anxiety and Despair: An Analysis of 'The Concept of Anxiety' and 'The Sickness unto Death.'" 1988. In *Dissertations (1962–2010)*. Access via Proquest Digital Dissertations. Paper AAI8904252.
Bonhoeffer, Dietrich. *Letters and Papers from Prison*. Edited by Eberhard Bethge. New York: Macmillan, 1953.
———. *The Cost of Discipleship*. New York: Macmillan, 1963.
Bracken, Joseph A. *Christianity and Process Thought*. Philadelphia: Templeton Foundation Press, 2006.
Bradford, M. Gerald. "William James on Religion and God: An Introduction to *The Varieties of Religious Experience*." No date or pages. Online: Maxwell Institute.byu.edu.
Briere, J., and S. Scott. *Principles of Trauma Therapy: A Guide to Symptoms, Evaluations, and Treatment*. Thousand Oaks, CA: Sage Publications, 2006.
Brown, Delwin, et al., eds. *Process Philosophy and Christian Thought*. New York: Bobbs-Merrill, 1971.
Browning, Don. *Religious Thought and the Modern Psychologies*. Philadelphia: Fortress Press, 1987.
Cobb, John B. "The Whiteheadian Doctrine of God." In *Process Philosophy and Christian Thought*, edited by Delwin Brown, et al. New York: Bobbs-Merrill, 1971.
———. "A Whiteheadian Christology." In *Process Philosophy and Christian Thought*, edited by Delwin Brown, et al. New York: Bobbs-Merrill, 1971.

Bibliography

Cobb, John B., and D. R. Griffin. *Process Theology: An Introductory Exposition.* Philadelphia: The Westminster Press, 1976.

Cozolino, Louis. *The Neuroscience of Psychotherapy.* New York: W.W. Norton, 2002.

Croft, H. A., and C. Parker. *I Always Sit with My Back to the Wall.* Stillpoint Media Services, 2011.

Cunningham, David S. "The Trinity." In *Postmodern Theology,* edited by K. J. Vanhoozer. Cambridge: University Press, 2003.

Deschner, John. "Austin Sermons." Unpublished sermon, 1976.

Dinkins, David B. *Narrative Pastoral Counseling.* Xulon Press, 2005.

Dodd, C. H. *Benefits of His Passion.* New York: Abingdon Press, no date.

Doehring, Carrie. *The Practice of Pastoral Care.* Louisville: Westminster John Knox Press, 2006.

Doud, Robert E. "Identity and Commitment." In *Religious Experience in Process Theology,* edited by H. J. Cargas and B. Lee. New York: Paulist Press, 1976.

Eliot, T. S. *The Cocktail Party.* New York: Harcourt, Brace, Jovanovich, 1950.

Ellis, George. "Intimations of Transcendence." In *Neuroscience and the Person,* edited by Robert John Russell, et al. Berkeley: Center for Theology and the Natural Sciences, 1999.

Fox, Matthew. *On Becoming a Musical Mystical Bear.* New York: Paulist Press, 1972.

Frost, Robert. *The Road Not Taken and Other Poems.* Mineola, NY: Dover Publications, 1993.

Gerkin, Charles. *The Living Human Document.* Nashville: Abingdon Press, 1984.

Goncalves, Oscar F. "Cognitive Narrative Psychotherapy: The Hermeneutic Construction of Alternative Meanings." In *Cognitive and Constructive Psychotherapies,* edited by M. J. Mahoney. New York: Springer, 1995.

Green, J. B. *The Circuit Rider,* September/October 2004.

Grenz, Stanley J. "The Social God and the Relational Self." In *Personal Identity in Theological Perspective,* edited by Richard Lints, et al. Grand Rapids: Eerdmans, 2006.

Griffin, David. "Creation out of Chaos and the Problem of Evil." In *Encountering Evil,* edited by S. T. Davis. Atlanta: John Knox Press, 1981.

Gula, R. M. "To Walk Together Again." Santa Rosa Hospital Newsletter, 2000.

Hartshorne, Charles. In John B. Cobb and D. R. Griffin, *Process Theology: An Introductory Exposition.* Philadelphia: Westminster Press, 1976.

———. *Omnipotence and Other Theological Mistakes.* Albany: State University of New York Press, 1984.

Hauerwas, Stanley. *With the Grain of the Universe.* Grand Rapids: Brazos Press, 2001.

Hawking, Stephen. *A Brief History of Time.* New York: Bantam Books, 1988.

———. *Into the Universe with Stephen Hawking.* Television documentary series. Created by Darlow Smithson Productions for the Discovery Channel. Premiered April 9, 2010.

Bibliography

Hill, E. W. "A Collaborative Pastoral Care and Counseling Supervisory Model." *The Journal of Pastoral Care* 55, no. 1, p. 77.

Hill, E. W., and P. M. Mullen. "Revisiting the Process Theology of Daniel Day Williams with Implications for Pastoral Care." *The Journal of Pastoral Care* 55, no. 2, pp. ##–##.

Hillman, James. *The Soul's Code.* New York: Warner Books, 1996.

Hobbs, Edward C., ed. *The Wesley Orders of Common Prayer.* The Board of Education of the Methodist Church, 1957.

Holder, Rodney. *The Heavens Declare.* W. Conshohocken, PA: Templeton Press, 2012.

James, William. *The Principles of Psychology.* Great Books of the Western World 53. Chicago: University of Chicago Press, 1952.

Keirsey, D., and M. Bates. *Please Understand Me: Character and Temperament Types.* Del Mar, CA: Prometheus Nemesis Book Co., 1984.

Knight, H. H. *The Circuit Rider,* September/October 2004.

Kopp, Sheldon. *If You Meet the Buddha on the Road, Kill Him!* Toronto: Bantam Books, 1972.

Latourette, K. S. *A History of Christianity.* New York: Harper and Brothers, 1953.

Lee, Bernard. *The Becoming of the Church.* New York: Paulist Press, 1974.

Lee, R. R., and J. C. Martin. *Psychotherapy after Kohut.* Hillsdale, NJ: The Analytic Press, 1991.

Lindbeck, George. *The Nature of Doctrine.* Louisville: Westminster John Knox Press, 1984.

Lonergan, Bernard. *Method in Theology.* New York: Herder and Herder, 1972.

Milbank, John. *Theology and Social Theory.* Oxford: Blackwell's, 1993.

Maxmen, J. S., and N. G. Ward. *Essential Psychopathology and Its Treatment.* New York: W. W. Norton Co., 1995.

Moore, Sebastian. *The Contagion of Jesus.* Maryknoll, NY: Orbis Books, 2007.

———. *The Fire and the Rose Are One.* New York: Seabury Press, 1981.

Newbigin, Lesslie. *Proper Confidence.* Grand Rapids: Eerdmans, 1995.

Niebuhr, Reinhold. *The Nature and Destiny of Man.* New York: Charles Scribner's Sons, 1953.

Nouwen, Henri J. M. *The Return of the Prodigal Son.* New York: Doubleday, 1992.

Ormerod, Neil. *Introducing Contemporary Theologies.* New York: Orbis Books, 1997

Otto, Rudolf. *The Idea of the Holy.* New York: Oxford University Press, 1923.

Outler, Albert. *John Wesley.* New York: Oxford University Press, 1964.

Pannenberg, Wolfhart. *Systematic Theology III.* Grand Rapids: Eerdmans, 1993.

Pargament, Kenneth. *Spiritually Integrated Psychotherapy.* New York: Guilford Press, 2007.

Peck, M. Scott. *People of the Lie.* New York: Simon and Schuster, 1983.

Peterson. Eugene H. *The Message.* Colorado Springs: NavPress, 2005.

Pittenger, Norman. *The Holy Spirit.* Philadelphia: United Church Press, 1974.

Bibliography

Platcher, William C. *The Triune God.* Louisville: Westminister John Knox Press, 2007.
Pope, Stephen J. "The Order of Love and Recent Catholic Ethics: A Constructive Proposal." *Theological Studies* 52 (1991), pp. ##–##.
Post, Stephen G. *Unlimited Love.* Philadelphia: The Templeton Foundation Press, 2003.
Rieger, Georg. *Theology from the Belly of the Whale.* Harrisburg: Trinity Press, 1999.
Rizzuto, Maria. *The Birth of the Living God.* Chicago: University of Chicago Press, 1979.
Rolnick, Philip. *Person, Grace, and God.* Grand Rapids: Eerdmans, 2007.
Rowe, C. E., and D. S. Mac Isaac. *Empathic Attunement.* Northvale, NJ: Jason Aronson, Inc., 1989.
Sable, Pat. *Attachment and Adult Psychotherapy.* Northvale, NJ: Jason Aronson, Inc., 2000.
Saddleback Valley Community Church website. "Celebrate Recovery." Online: www.saddleback.com/lakeforest/carehelp/celebraterecovery.
Scherer, Paul. *Love Is a Spendthrift.* New York: Harper and Brothers, 1961.
Schilpp, Paul A., ed. *The Philosophy of Alfred North Whitehead.* La Salle, IL: Open Court, 1941.
Sorenson, Randall L. *Minding Spirituality.* Hillsdale, NJ: The Analytic Press, 2004.
Tan, Siang-Yang. "Use of Prayer and Scripture in Cognitive-Behavioral Therapy." *Journal of Psychology and Christianity* 16, no. 2, pp. 101–111.
Tillich, Paul. *Shaking of the Foundations.* New York: Charles Scribner's Sons, 1948.
———. *Systematic Theology 1.* Chicago: University of Chicago Press, 1951.
———. *A History of Christian Thought.* New York: Harper and Row, 1968.
Townsend, L. L. *Introduction to Pastoral Counseling.* Nashville: Abingdon Press, 2009.
Travis, Stephen. *The Circuit Rider,* September/October 2004.
Volf, Miroslav. *Exclusion and Embrace.* Nashville: Abingdon Press, 1996.
Walker, Williston. *A History of the Christian Church.* New York: Charles Scribner's Sons, 1959.
Ward, Keith. *Religion and Revelation.* Oxford: Clarendon Press, 1994.
———. *God, Chance, and Necessity.* Rockport, MA: Oneworld Publications, 1996.
White, M., and D. Epston. *Narrative Means to Therapeutic Ends.* New York: W.W. Norton Co., 1990.
Wildman, W., and L. Brothers. "A Neurological-Semiotic Model of Religious Experiences." In *Neuroscience and the Person,* edited by Robert John Russell, et al. Berkeley: The Center for Theology and the Natural Sciences, 1999.
Williams, Daniel Day. *The Minister and the Care of Souls.* New York: Harper and Brothers, 1961.

Bibliography

———. *God's Grace and Man's Hope*. New York: Harper Chapel Books, 1965.
———. *The Spirit and the Forms of Love*. New York: Harper and Row, 1968.
———. *The Demonic and the Divine*. Minneapolis: Fortress Press, 1990.
Wise, Carroll. *Pastoral Psychotherapy: Theory and Practice*. New York: Jason Aronson, Inc., 1980.
Wright, N. T. *Simply Jesus*. New York: HarperCollins, 2011.
Zizioulas, John D. *Being as Communion*. Crestwood, NY: St. Vladimir's Seminary Press, 1985.
Zohar, Danah. *The Quantum Self*. New York: William Morrow, 1990.

www.ingramcontent.com/pod-product-compliance
Lightning Source LLC
Chambersburg PA
CBHW070920160426
43193CB00011B/1540